$19.95

W9-AXW-176

Maps *of the* Shaker West

A collection of maps and histories
of better known and lesser known
Shaker sites in Kentucky, Ohio,
Indiana, Illinois, and Michigan
beginning in 1800.

Maps *of the* Shaker West
A Journey of Discovery

Knot Garden Press
Dayton, Ohio

Martha Boice
Dale Covington
Richard Spence

Copyright © 1997
Knot Garden Press
7712 Eagle Creek Drive
Dayton, Ohio 45459

All rights reserved. No part of this publication may be
reproduced, stored in a retrieval system, or transmitted,
in any form or by any means, electronic, mechanical,
photocopying, recording, or otherwise, without the
prior written permission of the copyright owner.

First Edition

ISBN:0-9655018-1-7

Ruth Leonard Design

C & O Printing, Inc.

Contents

List of Illustrations

List of Maps

Maps *of the* Shaker West

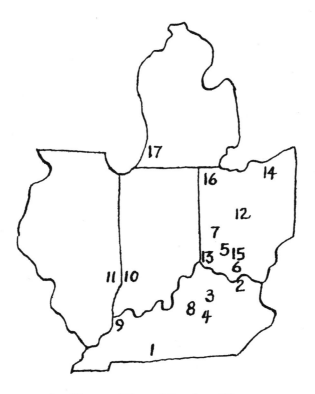

1 Gasper River Meeting House
   and South Union, Kentucky

2 Cabin Creek, Kentucky

3 Cane Ridge, Kentucky

4 Paint Lick, Kentucky

5 Union Village, Ohio

6 Eagle Creek and Straight Creek, Ohio

7 Watervliet, Ohio

8 Pleasant Hill, Kentucky

9 Red Banks, Kentucky

10 West Union, Indiana

11 Ambrau, Illinois

12 Darby Plains, Ohio

13 White Water, Ohio

14 North Union, Ohio

15 Clinton County, Ohio

16 Henry County, Ohio

17 Berrien Springs, Michigan

Acknowledgments

This book started its life as a group of maps created by the Western Shaker Study Group for participants of the Berkshire Shaker Seminar coming "West" in 1993. While there was an attempt to verify locations and to check history books and deeds, this collection of maps turned out to be just the beginning of our search for the Shaker West.

We have made our maps more accurate in portraying the establishment of Shakerism in the West with the help of many people. The Kentucky Transportation Cabinet gave us permission to use their county maps. Franklin McGuire assisted with the Cane Ridge map. The Henderson County Genealogical and Historical Society helped us locate Red Banks in Henderson. Don Janzen located the cemetery for the Paint Lick Meeting House.

Research for the Eagle Creek and Straight Creek Shaker locations required an intense effort. The Ohio Historical Society Library provided Virginia Military Surveys. The Recorders Office for Adams County and the Brown County Genealogical Society, especially Dorothy Helton, Eva Mae Davis, Martha Telaneus, and Ruth Arnott, helped to fill in the gaps in our information. James Newman helpfully pointed out that some Brown County deeds might be located among the Clermont County records.

Members of the Western Shaker Study Group willingly provided accounts and information. Sharon Edwards and Mary Lue Warner were consulted about Union Village. Rose Mary Lawson and Bill Mooney collaborated on Watervliet. The Pleasant Hill account was written by Jean Dones.

Larrie Curry, curator at Pleasant Hill, provided her fine line drawings as well as answers to many questions. Susan Hughes, Phillipa Burgess and Dr. Kate Covington helped to locate Holy Sinai's Plain on the Pleasant Hill map. Connie Mills of the Kentucky Library of Western Kentucky University meticulously documented references to the manuscript pages in *South Union Record A*. Donna Parker, Tommy Hines, Dale Spencer, Eloise Hadden, and Mike Sisk filled out the picture of South Union in a significant way. Eddie Belle Denison and Dorothy Steers assisted with deed research for South Union.

For sharing their knowledge about the only Shaker community in Indiana, we are grateful to Dorothy Jones, John Martin Smith, and Don Janzen.

The Darby Plains Shakers in Union County, Ohio, seemed impossible to decipher until John Bry of Urbana said, "We had a group of Shakers in Champaign County," and the mysteries began to unfold. Rachel Robinson of Milford Center, Morse family researchers Lois Barr and Mike Morse, and writer Trella H. Romine supplied answers to knotty problems. The Westfall family and Randy Poland graciously gave us a wonderful tour of Champaign and Union County Farnhamite and Shaker sites.

Rose Mary Lawson, Cathie Winans, Mary Jo Groppe, and map researcher Augusta Thomas provided much information about North Union in Shaker Heights.

It was Richard M. Helwig, Sunbury, Ohio, director of the Center for Ghost Town Research in Ohio, who alerted us to Shaker ownership of land in Henry County, Ohio. Serving as a thoughtful and knowledgeable guide for a tour of Shaker properties in Henry County, Genevieve Eicher also shared family lore, archaeological reports, and charts from that county. Elizabeth Shaver, Troy, New York, carefully documented information about the Watervliet, New York, Shaker who owned that land.

Darlene and George Kohrman from Portage, Marilyn Baumgras of Laingsburg, and Scott and Mary Ellen Pluss of Berrien Springs, all active in the Michigan Shaker Study Group, provided their files on the Berrien Springs Shaker Farm and other sites in Michigan. Stephen Paterwic helped to relate the happenings at Berrien Springs to the events at New Lebanon, New York.

Others who assisted with the project include Mary Allen, Melba Hunt, and Jack Sutton. We gratefully thank those who read all or part of the text, including Stephen Paterwic, Nick Apple, Ruth B. Oake, and Carl Becker.

Even the trio who produced this book assisted each other. Martha made presentations about the project at historical meetings and shared with Dale and Richard stacks of deeds, surveys, and local maps that she unearthed. Dale provided useful reference articles and census lists as well as writing and editorial help. He combed a variety of records in compiling the story of South Union. Richard left his drawing board to hike over the lands at Watervliet, Ohio, pacing distances and sketching terrain features. He also contributed to the sections for White Water and Union Village. It has been truly a group project.

Our gratitude for all the generous assistance we have received knows no bounds.

The Beginnings

All Shaker roads lead from Manchester, England. After suffering much for her religious views, Mother Ann Lee left Manchester with a small band of eight followers in 1774. She had visions which told her that her religion would flourish in America. Her small group eventually settled near Albany, New York, in a place called Watervliet by the local Dutch settlers. Originally known as the United Society of Believers in Christ's Second Appearing, the sect's name became shortened to "Shakers" because of the exuberant shaking and jerking which were an integral part of their worship.

The Shakers spread their religion and gained converts throughout New England, capitalizing on the revivals among various religious groups. In 1805 this missionary effort was directed to the "West" when news reached the Shaker Central Ministry of similar revivals there. In those days Kentucky, Ohio, Indiana, Michigan, and Illinois were part of a developing and largely unsettled land called the West.

In Kentucky the Presbyterians and other churches held camp meetings, gathering many people together for amazing religious experiences. The first revival occured at Gasper, Kentucky, in Logan County in 1800. Such was its strength that the religious fervor spread across Kentucky and even into southwestern Ohio. These widely separated camp meetings and outdoor worship festivals are known as the Kentucky Revival.

Shaker missionaries from the East attended these camp meetings and used them as an opportunity to establish Shaker congregations. According to Shaker chronicler J.P. MacLean, "Where a camp-meeting was advertised, a Shaker missionary promptly made his appearance, and lost no opportunity to instill his doctrines."[1] The first Shaker community to become established was Union Village in Lebanon, Ohio (1805). The missionaries extended their work to Eagle Creek and Straight Creek in Adams and Clermont Counties, Ohio (1805), to Watervliet near Dayton, Ohio (1806), Pleasant Hill, Kentucky (1806), South Union, Kentucky (1807), and West Union, also called Busro, Indiana (1807). North Union and White Water, both in Ohio, were begun in 1822. Union Village became the lead community in the West.

Starting with the demise of West Union in 1827 and North Union in 1889, all the major Western Shaker communities were vacated by 1922 when South Union closed. Because of their early formation and short duration, little is known of the smaller Western Shaker communities such as Eagle Creek and Darby Plains.

This book presents maps of the Western Shaker sites. You will find directional maps and many drawings by Richard Spence. Computer generated maps of the sites (except White Water) relate the Shaker holdings to modern maps and were crafted by the skilled hands of Dale Covington. Martha Boice provided the narrative (with assistance from those named throughout the text) and research.

In the footnotes those manuscripts held by the Western Reserve Historical Society and available on microfilm are designated WRHS and listed as they appear in Kermit J. Pike's *A Guide to Shaker Manuscripts* (Cleveland: Western Reserve Historical Society, 1974).

The proceeds from this book will be used to provide historical markers for the Shaker communities in southwestern Ohio through the auspices of the Western Shaker Study Group.

---

[1] J.P. MacLean, *Shakers of Ohio* (1907; reprint, Philadelphia: Porcupine Press, 1975), 272.

FARM
DEACON'S
SHOP
Shaker Village

Larrie Spier Curry

*Farm Deacon's Shop
Pleasant Hill, Ky.*

Chapter 1

The Kentucky Revival

After the Revolutionary War, the lands to the West, including Kentucky, Ohio, and Indiana, were open for settlement. This wild and unsettled land had few roads, only the beginnings of government, and very few churches.

The occasional minister who came along with the tide of migration often suffered discouragement in serving the religious needs of the scattered population.

It was different with members of John Rankin's church near the Gasper River in Logan County, Kentucky. In his journal, Rankin described a meeting in June 1800 where several preachers spoke with a large gathering. Usually these services lasted several hours. After the preaching some left for home; others remained in their seats contemplating. "But," writes Rankin, "wonderful to be seen & heard; on a sudden, an alarming cry burst from the midst of the deepest silence; some were thrown into wonderful & strange contortions of features, body & limbs frightful to the beholder others had singular gestures with words & actions quite inconsistent with presbyterial order & usage—all was alarm & confusion for the moment." There was a feeling of confidence in the preachers that "this was a work of God. . . .a mighty effusion of his spirit."[1]

Barton W. Stone, the Presbyterian minister at Cane Ridge, Kentucky, struggling with the doctrines taught in the Confession of Faith, heard about a camp meeting in the spring of 1801 in Logan County. Wanting to experience the power of religion, Stone attended the camp meeting. He described its powerful effect:

> *The multitudes came together, and continued a number of days and nights encamped on the ground; during which time worship was carried on in some part of the encampment. The scene to me was new, and passing strange. . . .Many, very many fell down, as men slain in battle, and continued for hours in an apparently breathless and motionless state—sometimes for a few moments reviving, and exhibiting symptoms of life by a deep groan, or piercing shriek, or by a prayer for mercy most fervently uttered. After lying thus four hours, they obtained deliverance. . . .Gradually. . .they would rise shouting deliverance, and then would address the surrounding multitude in language truly eloquent and impressive.[2]*

This was the beginning of the Kentucky Revival. Camp meetings spread to other Kentucky communities, as well as Ohio and Tennessee, in response to the awakened religious hunger of the new settlers. Richard McNemar described the terrible and awesome power of the revivals held in central and northern Kentucky in his book, *The Kentucky Revival*, published in Cincinnati in 1807. McNemar, a well-trained Presbyterian theologian who was able to read Greek, Latin, and Hebrew, became a leading influence in Western Shakerism. The sites he describes for these revivals include Cabin Creek, Concord, Paint Lick, Cane Ridge, Indian Creek, Pleasant Point, and Red Banks in Kentucky, and Eagle Creek in Ohio.

East Family Dwelling
Pleasant Hill, Ky.

---

1 *South Union Shaker Record A*, 1805-1836, 29-30, Kentucky Library, Western Kentucky University. The first part of *Shaker Record A* is an autobiographical account of John Rankin, written in 1845. Another section includes the diary of Benjamin Seth Youngs. Between the text and notes, both the manuscript page number and date will be given for quotations from this important journal.

2 Elder John Rogers, *The Biography of Eld. Barton Warren Stone, Written by Himself: with Additions and Reflections* (Cincinnati, J.A. and U.P. James, 1847), 34-35.

Chapter 2

Gasper River Meeting House
Logan County, Kentucky

Revival activities began at the Gasper River Meeting House which its pastor, John Rankin, described vaguely as located five miles below South Union. This first site has not been identified. The site of the second meetinghouse, built in July 1800, was located one and a half miles from South Union on the Clear Fork of the Gasper River. This building was finished just in time for the first camp meeting to which families came in their wagons, encamping on the grounds.

John Rankin described the preparations for that memorable gathering. "We had finished shingling the new meeting house the evening previous, & scattered the shavings over the floor to prevent the dust from soiling the peoples clothes, & made temporary seats."[1]

Rankin portrayed the meeting on that warm July day:

> *On Friday morning at an early hour, the people began to assemble in large numbers from every quarter, & by the usual hour for preaching to commence, there was a multitude collected, unprecedented in this or any other new country of so sparse a population. The rising ground to the west & south of the meeting house, was literally lined with covered wagons & other appendages—each one furnished with provisions & accommodations, suitable to make them comfortable on the ground during the solemnity. When I came in view of this vast assemblage with their new & singular preparations which they had made to qualify them to attend & sustain the meeting without interruption to themselves or others, I was astonished!*[2]

When Rankin and some 20 to 30 members of his congregation embraced Shakerism, those who were left united with other congregations in the area. The Gasper River Meeting House fell into disuse from 1811 to 1838. With just a few members, it became associated with other congregations in the area. Eastern Shakers who wished to see the site of the origination of the Kentucky Revival made the Meeting House a point of interest in their travels.[3] For example, Amos Stewart of New Lebanon, New York, came in 1852. He wrote in his journal: "The roof has fell in, but the logs stand quite erect, it was quite a large building perhaps 35 by 50 feet about 10 feet high, a door on the south side and one on each end. A grave yard but a few rods distant all in the woods [sic] some new graves."[4]

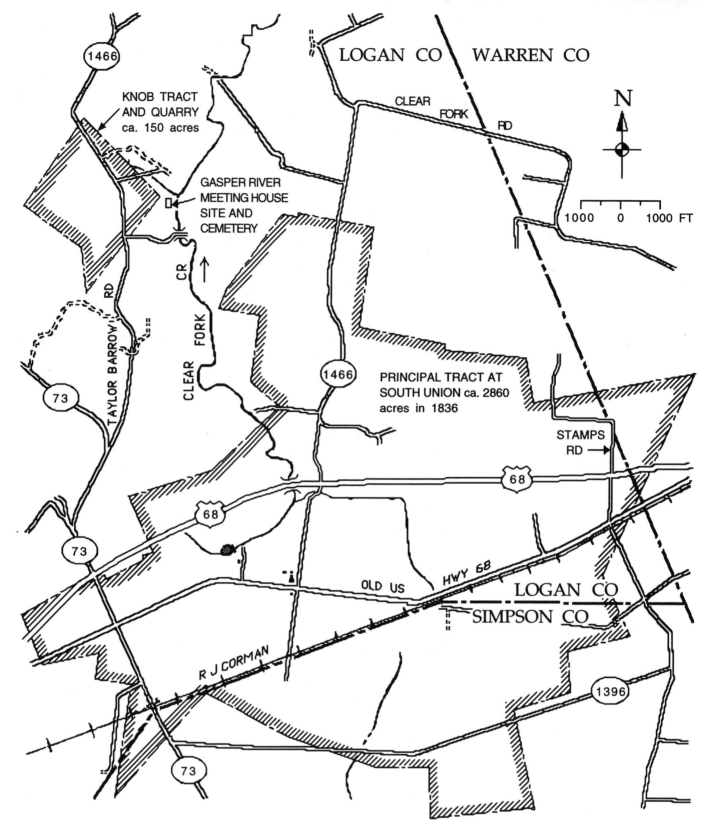

GASPER RIVER MEETING HOUSE SITE
AND SOUTH UNION TRACTS NEARBY

[1] *South Union Record A*, "Autobiography," 31-32.

[2] Ibid.

[3] Br. Thomas Whitaker, "The Gasper River Meeting House," *The Filson Club History Quarterly* 56 (1982): 58.

[4] Amos Steward, *Journal of a Visit to the Western Communities*, WRHS V:B-150, July 22, 1852, 108.

Chapter 3

Cabin Creek

Lewis County, Kentucky

The Presbyterians at Cabin Creek met in a small log house. This congregation thrived under the leadership of Richard McNemar who served as pastor of the church from the fall of 1797 to the spring of 1802.[1]

An important camp meeting which awakened this congregation occured May 22, 1801. It continued for four days and three nights, with

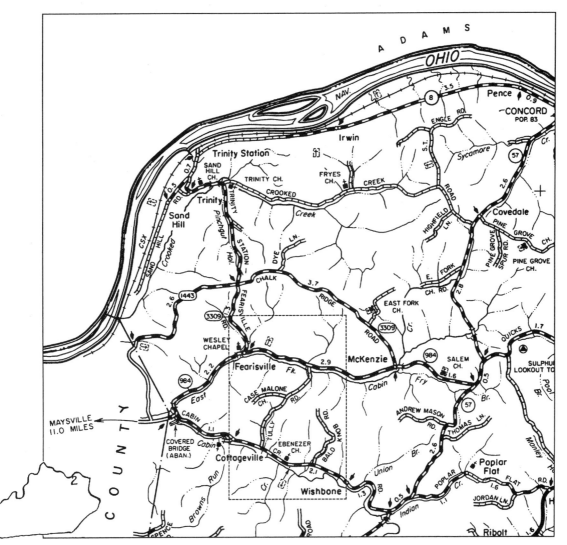

Lewis County, Kentucky   *Kentucky Transportation Cabinet*

participants sensing a supernatural power at work. McNemar chronicled the event in his book, *The Kentucky Revival*:

> *No circumstance at this meeting, appeared more striking, than the great numbers that fell on the third night: and to prevent their being trodden under foot by the multitude, they were collected together and laid out in order, on two squares of the meetinghouse; which, like so many dead corpses, covered a considerable part of the floor.— There were persons at this meeting from Caneridge, Concord, Eagle-Creek, and other neighboring congregations, who partook of the spirit of the work, which was a particular means of its spreading.[2]*

Southwestern Ohio and Lewis County, Kentucky

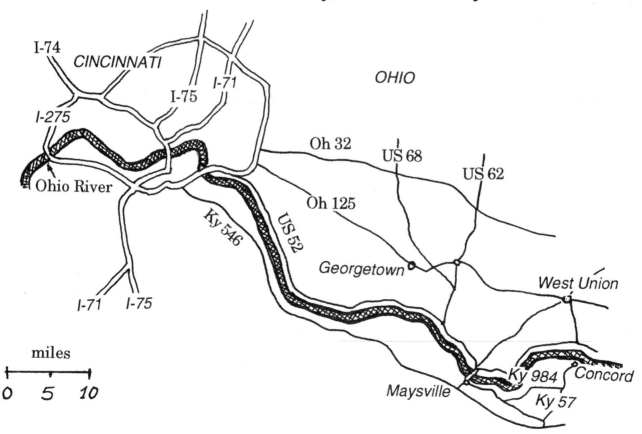

There were persons at this meeting from Caneridge, Concord, Eagle-Creek, and other neighboring congregations...

By the fall of 1801, some of the leaders of the Cabin Creek congregation brought charges of heresy against McNemar to the Presbytery. They felt that "he began. . .in his preaching to deviate from the doctrines contained in the Confession of Faith of the Presbyterian church."[3] The charges were dropped and McNemar moved on to minister to the Presbyterian congregation at Turtle Creek, four miles west of Lebanon, Ohio, in the spring of 1802.

Those at Cabin Creek who were loyal to McNemar's beliefs became known as "The New School Presbyterians" or "The New Lights." They continued to meet in the small log house called the Camp Spring Meeting House. Those who wanted to follow the strict Calvanist teachings of the church withdrew from this congregation and erected a church building farther up the creek and named it Ebenezer.[4] It is still along Cabin Creek Road two miles east of an abandoned covered bridge. The Camp Spring Meeting House was on Route 984 (Fearisville Road) just east of Trinity Station-Fearisville Road. The church cemetery still stands on the north side of the road.

By continuting east on Route 984 and turning north (left) on Route 57, it is just ten miles to Concord, another site that was part of the Kentucky Revival.

---

[1] Clara Degman Hook, "Cabin Creek's Contribution to the Early Religious History of America," *Lewis County (Kentucky) Herald*, October 12, 1939.

[2] Richard McNemar, *The Kentucky Revival* (1807; reprint, Albany [Cincinnati]: E. and E. Hosford, 1808), 24.

[3] J.P. MacLean., *Life of Richard McNemar* (Franklin, Ohio: The Franklin Chronicle, 1905), 8.

[4] Hook, *Lewis County Herald*.

Chapter 4

Cane Ridge

Bourbon County, Kentucky

The largest revival took place at Cane Ridge a few months after the Cabin Creek Revival. Barton W. Stone arrived in 1796 from North Carolina to become a temporary pastor for the Presbyterian church at Cane Ridge, as well as nearby Concord. The Cane Ridge Meeting House was built in 1791.

August 6, 1801, marked the beginning of the great Cane Ridge revival. The camp meeting lasted for five days and four nights. The number of people collected on the ground at once was supposed to be about 20,000, but it was thought a much greater number were there in the course of the meeting. The encampment consisted of 135 wheel carriages and tents consistent with the number of people attending. A large tent was erected in a clearing; around it were laid off streets for tents and vehicles.[1]

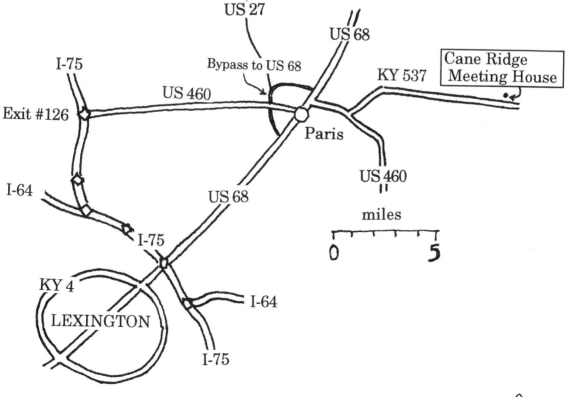

Robert W. Finley, an early minister at Cane Ridge (1793-1795), reported: "The scene was awful, beyond description—the ranges of tents, the fires reflecting light amidst the swaying branches of the trees, the hundreds of persons moving to and fro,—singing, praying, shouting from different parts of the grounds like the sounds of many rushing waters, was enough to swallow up all powers of contemplation. Such as tried to escape conviction by leaving were frequently struck down upon the way and compelled to return of their own accord."[2]

CANE RIDGE MEETING HOUSE
— 1791 —

"The scene was awful, beyond description—
the ranges of tents, the fires reflecting light
amidst the swaying branches of the trees, the
hundreds of persons moving to and fro..."

[1] R. Carlyle Buley, *The Old Northwest* (1950; reprint, Bloomington: Indiana University Press, 1978), 2:422.

[2] Hook, *Lewis County Herald.*

Chapter 5

The Springfield Presbytery

The force of the revivals became a disquieting part of religious life in Kentucky and Ohio. Parishioners from Cabin Creek brought heresy charges against Richard McNemar at a meeting of the Presbytery of Springdale. (The meeting was held in what is now northern Cincinnati.) The Presbytery heard the charges but did not find any substantiation for them. In September 1803, however, further charges came forth at the synod meeting in Lexington.

Several ministers felt that the Presbyterian Church did not allow for freedom of spiritual inquiry and they wanted to remove the layers of church hierarchy. Their belief was that each church member had to develop his own inner light. "New Lights" became the name given to those who wanted an emphasis on individual spirituality rather than the heavy Calvinistic creed of predestination.

At the Synod meeting at Lexington representing most of the Presbyterian Churches in Kentucky, Barton W. Stone, John Dunlavy, Robert Marshall, John Thompson, and Richard McNemar all withdrew and formed their own Springfield Presbytery within the folds of the church on September 10, 1803. The Synod told this group of ministers they could not break away from the parent church. They assured the Synod, however, that they had already formed their own group.[1]

Not quite a year had gone by when it became obvious to this small group of ministers that their Presbytery had created a schism within the Presbyterian Church, a result they had not foreseen nor desired. They returned to the church at Cane Ridge to dissolve their Springfield Presbytery, creating a document they called "The Last Will and Testament of the Springfield Presbytery." Their alliance ended on June 28, 1804. (See Appendix I.)

What happened to those who signed this document? David Purviance, who was an assistant to Barton Stone at Cane Ridge, wrote in his autobiography that "the Shakers carried off Richard McNemar and John Dunlavy." Robert Marshall and John Thompson eventually wrote enough about the error of their ways in becoming a part of the New Light Church to pave the way for their return to the Presbyterian Church. Barton W. Stone

Their belief was that each church member had to develop his own inner light.

continued to develop the Christian Church in Kentucky and Ohio. Cane Ridge Church near Paris, Kentucky, is a tribute to this organizer and founder of the Christian Church.

David Purviance continued his ministry in the Christian Church, serving a congregation in New Paris, Ohio, north of Dayton. He felt that the Shakers had done a service to the Presbyterian church by taking some of the radical fringe.[2]

---

[1] Elder Levi Purviance, *The Biography of Elder David Purviance* (Dayton: B.R. & G.W. Ells, 1848), 40.
[2] Ibid., 115.

Chapter 6

Paint Lick

Garrard County, Kentucky

Having heard reports in the newspapers about the amazing revivals in Kentucky and Ohio, Mother Lucy Wright at New Lebanon, New York, the lead Shaker community, decided to send missionaries to that wild Western part of civilization. On New Year's morning, 1805, John Meachan, Issachar Bates, and Benjamin Seth Youngs set out on foot, sharing one horse to carry their luggage.

By early March they had reached Matthew Houston's at Paint Lick, Garrard County, Kentucky. Benjamin Seth Youngs wrote: "Thursday, March 7, 1805. First Public testimony of the gospel in the western Country. At Paint Lick Meeting House we publickly opened the testimony today, to Matthew Houston's congregation." In copying these entries later at South Union, Harvey Eades added: "Matthew Houston was a public Minister of the Presbyterian Church, and afterwards among the New Lights & continued a public ministry to the world during his earth life."[1]

It was almost a year later that Peggy Houston, Matthew's wife, confessed to Benjamin and became a Shaker. The next day Matthew Houston joined along with his competent servant, Isaac Newton, who was part Indian.

In May 1806, Youngs recorded: "In the woods near Matthews from 600 to 800 people assembled. Benjamin spoke 3 hours, standing on a log and the people sat on rails. He discoursed on Salvation from all sin - The Resurrection & judgment - Matthew testified his faith in & fellowship with all that had been said."[2]

By 1808 the converts from Paint Lick were moving to Union Village and nearby Pleasant Hill. Matthew Houston and his family made their permanent home at Union Village.

The Paint Lick Meeting House was located southwest of the town of Paint Lick on Manse Road near Route 52. The cemetery on that road still marks the site. To travel to Paint Lick from Pleasant Hill, see the directional map on page 49.

---

[1] *South Union Record A*, May 25. 1806, 42. At Union Village Houston served as an elder in the Center House or the First Order during the 1830s and assisted with the leadership of the community until his death in 1853.

[2] Ibid., 62.

*"At Paint Lick Meeting House we publickly opened
the testimony today, to Matthew Houston's congregation."*

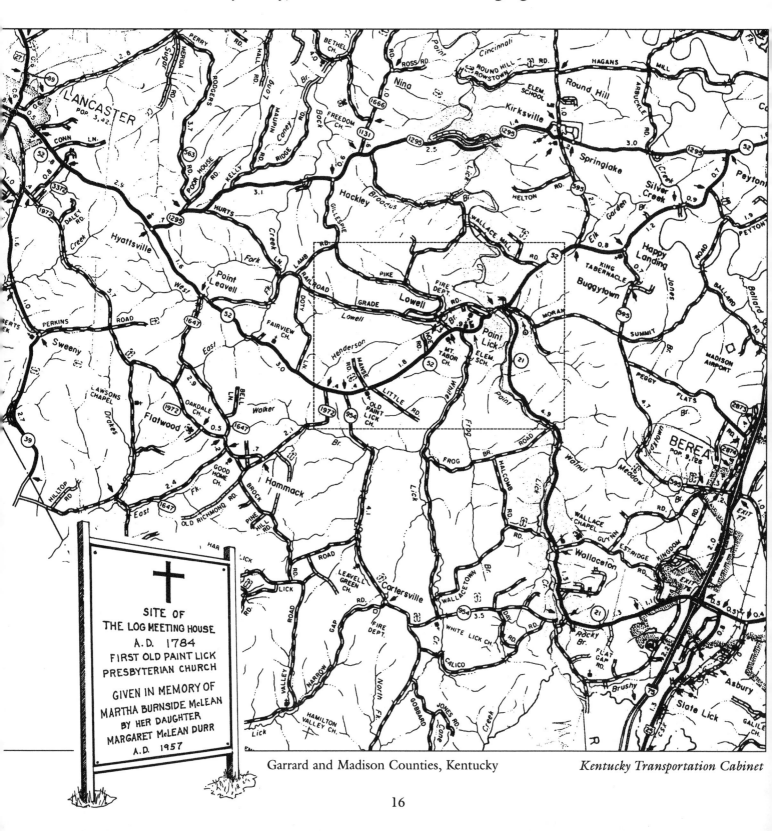

Garrard and Madison Counties, Kentucky

Kentucky Transportation Cabinet

Chapter 7

Union Village
Warren County, Ohio

Meeting House at Union Village, Ohio

Ohio had been a state not quite two years when the three Shaker missionaries arrived at Warren County's first permanent settlement, Beedle Station. William Beedle's blockhouse, built to protect early settlers, served as the center of the settlement. Most of the Beedle family were strong Calvinistic Presbyterians. They had built the nearby Turtle Creek Church to which Rev. James Kemper had served as minister by traveling from Cincinnati until he was replaced in 1802 by the New Light preacher from Kentucky, Richard McNemar.

The Shaker missionaries, as recorded in Issachar Bates' diary: "arrived on the 22 day of March 1805 at Malcolm Worleys where we found the first rest for the soles of our feet having traveled 1,233 miles in two months and twenty-two days. Here we were received with the greatest kindness altho utter strangers."[1] Malcolm Worley, a member of McNemar's church and a prominent land owner, adopted the Shaker faith on March 27, 1805, becoming the first Shaker convert in the West. Worley's conversion was quickly followed by the conversions of his neighbors, McNemar and Beedle. Such was the leadership of these men that the entire Turtle Creek congregation followed them into the Shaker faith.

5

All the Shakers in the West looked to Union Village for guidance.

This group served as the nucleus for the Shaker community called Union Village. Worley's quarter section became the Centre Family; McNemar's, the East Family. The Shaker Central Ministry at New Lebanon, New York, then sent a small cadre of Eastern Shakers headed by Elder David Darrow and Eldress Ruth Farrington to take charge of the new Believers.

Union Village grew rapidly from 1805 to 1830 in membership, acreage, industries, and buildings. By 1818, 634 Shakers lived in eleven families. Eight great dwelling houses were built, of which two survive.[2]

Shaker Creek (called Dicks Creek on Richard McNemar's ca. 1806 map) was dammed in four places as it went through the property, creating millponds to power a grist mill, saw mills, a fulling mill, and an oil mill. In addition to raising sheep, hogs, and thoroughbred Durham cattle, the Union Village Shakers produced linen for themselves and linseed oil to sell. The Shakers found widespread markets for their garden seeds, medicinal herbs, and broomcorn. Shaker peddlers sold preserves, knitted goods, and palm-leaf bonnets. Other industries included brick making and pottery.[3]

As remarkable as Union Village's agriculture and industries were, the strength of the village was in its early leadership. It served as the overseeing organization for the Western communities, tirelessly seeking to expand Shakerism into Ohio, Kentucky, Indiana, and in later years, Georgia. All the Shakers in the West looked to Union Village for guidance. The names of the other communities, North Union, West Union, and South Union, reflect their physical orientation to Union Village as well.

The year 1835 was very difficult for Union Village. Caterpillars attacked and destroyed many trees. Then nine inches of rain fell within a few hours, flooding the Shakers' lowlands and destroying their mill-dams and oil mill as well as clothing, fulling, and coloring shops, doing an estimated $25,000 in damage. In June, Trustee Nathan Sharp absconded with a horse and a large amount of money. He married another defecting Shaker, Charlotte Morrell, in October. Sharp managed the Green Tree Tavern, located near the northern boundary of Union Village.[4] You may still see this reminder of a shocking defection at 1660 State Route 741 and Greentree Road.

In 1865 the Old North House with its tin shop, broom shop, carpenter shop, shoemaker shop, and sarsaparilla laboratory, was lost to fire. In the 1860s and 1870s several land purchases added to the community's

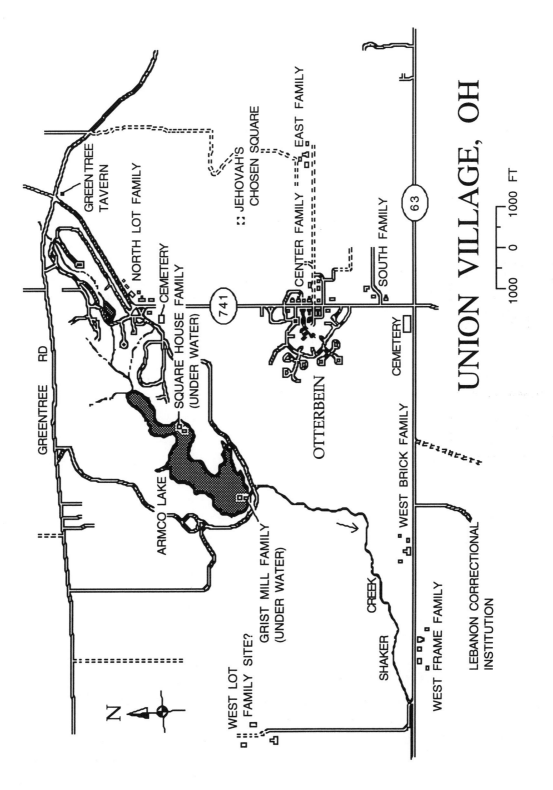

UNION VILLAGE, OH

GREENTREE RD

GREENTREE TAVERN

NORTH LOT FAMILY

CEMETERY

SQUARE HOUSE FAMILY
(UNDER WATER)

:: JEHOVAH'S
CHOSEN SQUARE

CENTER FAMILY

EAST FAMILY

ARMCO LAKE

SOUTH FAMILY

OTTERBEIN

GRIST MILL FAMILY
(UNDER WATER)

CEMETERY

WEST LOT
FAMILY SITE?

WEST BRICK FAMILY

SHAKER CREEK

WEST FRAME FAMILY

LEBANON CORRECTIONAL
INSTITUTION

741

63

N

1000   0   1000 FT

debt without providing much income. In 1877 a bank in Lebanon failed and the Shakers lost their account of more than $7,500. A loan of $16,000 to the Dayton Furnace Company was a total loss, the work of a dishonest lawyer.[5] Trustee James Fennessee worked tirelessly to reduce Union Village's indebtedness.

Elder Joseph R. Slingerland, a Shaker physician from Mount Lebanon, New York, was appointed trustee and assumed responsibility for the leadership of Union Village in 1890. By this time buildings were in need of repairs. Early in his ministry Slingerland made radical improvements to the 1810 Center House. Seven kinds of marble were used in the floors. A slate roof, Victorian towers, and porches created what looked like an entirely new building. Even this effort, known as Marble Hall, failed to attract new members.

It was Elder Slingerland who directed the acquisition of nearly 15,000 acres on the Georgia coast in 1898. Two small bands of Shakers, mostly from Union Village, attempted to establish fresh, appealing colonies—first on the plantations of Altama and Hopeton near Brunswick and then on a large plantation at White Oak.[6] White Oak residents saw their Shaker neighbors let a contract for a large dwelling house, raise range-fed cattle, and harvest crops of corn, pumpkins, sweet potatoes, and other garden vegetables. However the colonization efforts soon ended. Few new converts and unbearable debts arising from the Georgia ventures and other speculations led to a change in leadership at Union Village in 1901 and sale of the Shaker lands in Georgia shortly afterwards.

By 1909 the number of Shakers at Union Village had dwindled to 26. The Central Ministry at Mount Lebanon, New York, put the 4,500-acre village with more than 100 buildings on the market.[7] For the next three years various groups and organizations vied to purchase Union Village from the Shakers. On October 15, 1912, the Church of the United Brethren in Christ signed a land contract with the Shakers, taking title to the property on March 5, 1913. The entire property sold for $325,000.

At this time 16 Shakers remained. While the United Brethren Church converted the Shaker buildings into facilities for an orphanage and old folks' home, it reserved one of the Shaker buildings, Marble Hall, as a home for the remaining Union Village Shakers during the next 10 years. Four or five younger Shaker women from Canterbury, New Hampshire, were always

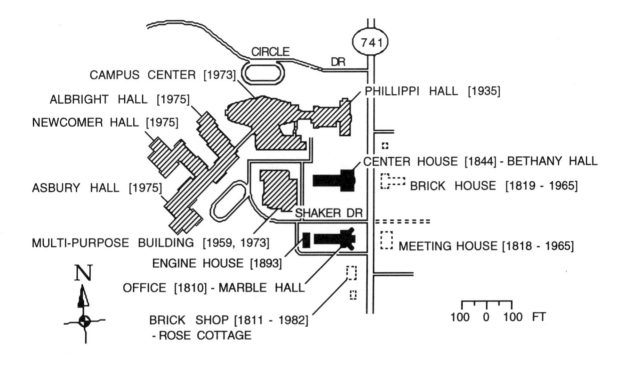

Principal Buildings at Center Family Site

present to care for the elderly Shakers at Union Village. By June 1920, 10 of the 16 Shakers had died and were buried in a plot in the Lebanon cemetery. The last three men left the Society; the last three sisters moved to Canterbury. Their departure ended the Shakers' presence in Ohio.

Most of the land which once made up the village is shared by Otterbein-Lebanon, a large United Methodist retirement community, which has much of its 1,500 acres under cultivation; a recreational park operated by the employees of AK Steel Corporation, formerly Armco Steel, Inc.; two maximum security state prisons; a county prison; and an Ohio Department of Transportation facility.

Richard Spence

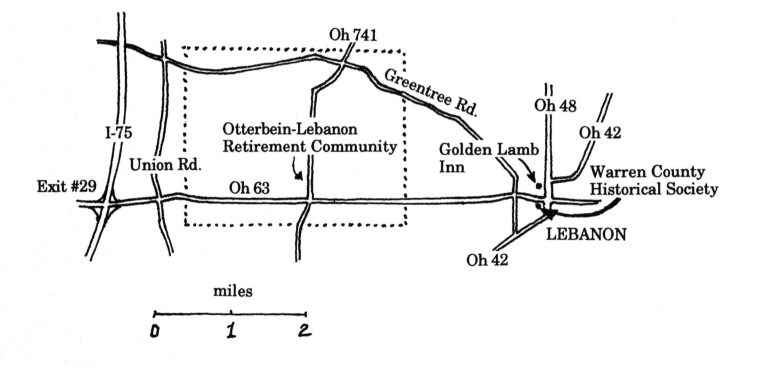

Malcolm Worley...adopted the Shaker faith on March 27, 1805, becoming the first Shaker convert in the West.

To Visit Union Village

Three Union Village buildings are part of the campus at Otterbein-Lebanon. In addition to Marble Hall, the 1844 Center Family dwelling (now Bethany Hall) and an 1893 Engine House are visible from State Route 741. Museum areas, which include two downstairs rooms and a full attic in Marble Hall, can be visited to view Shaker furniture and artifacts including some farming implements. Of particular interest is the three-story water holding tank visible in the attic of Marble Hall. Call (513) 932-1607 or (513) 932-2020 to make an appointment for a tour.

The Warren County Historical Society, 105 South Broadway in downtown Lebanon, displays its collection of Shaker furniture in room settings. Many pieces of Western Shaker furniture from Otterbein-Lebanon combine with Eastern pieces in the collection to tell the story of Union Village. A special wing, the Robert and Virginia Jones Gallery, using the Shaker principle of borrowed light, is the setting for this outstanding collection. The museum is open Tuesday through Saturday, 9 A.M. to 4 P.M., Sundays, NOON to 4 P.M. (Closed Mondays and holidays.) The Rocking Horse Gift Shop has an excellent selection of Shaker reproductions and books. Phone: (513) 932-1817.

A Shaker visit to Lebanon would be incomplete without a tour, a meal, or even an overnight stay at the Golden Lamb Inn, 27-31 South Broadway. It is Ohio's oldest inn and has hosted many dignitaries. Dine in the Shaker Room on the first floor amid Shaker artifacts collected by former inn owner Robert Jones. An herb cabinet from Watervliet, Ohio, is on a shelf above the stairs from the first to the second floor. Your stamina will be rewarded if you climb to the fourth floor to view two display rooms of Shaker furniture. Keep your eyes open for Shaker pieces as your tour the building and shop in the downstairs gift shop. Don't forget to order Sister Lizzie's Shaker Sugar Pie or Ohio Lemon Pie for dessert. Phone: (513) 932-5065.

1 *A Concise Sketch of the Life and Experiences of Isachar Bates, Written by Himself,* Manuscript Collection, Dayton and Montgomery County Public Library, Dayton, Ohio, 39.

2 *1810 Centre House* (Marble Hall), 1819 Brick House, 1819 West Brick House, 1823 North Lot House, 1824 North House, 1826 Office, *1844 Brick House* (Bethany Hall), 18— — South House.

3 Sharon E. Edwards, "Brooms, Looms and Flumes: Union Village Industry, 1805-1870," *Union Village Seminar* (Lebanon, Ohio: Warren County Historical Society, 1989), 10-12.

4 Hazel Spencer Phillips, *Richard the Shaker* (Lebanon, Ohio: Published by the author, 1972), 108.

5 MacLean, *Shakers of Ohio,* 101-109.

6 Dale W. Covington, "Union Village and the Shaker Colonies in Georgia," *Union Village Seminar,* 17-21.

7 The name Mount Lebanon was used for the New Lebanon Shaker community after 1861.

Chapter 8

Eagle Creek and Straight Creek

Adams, Brown, and Clermont Counties, Ohio

The spirit of the Kentucky Revival reached into Ohio and touched the congregation at Eagle Creek. The year was 1801 and meetings at nearby Cabin Creek and Concord, Kentucky, created great excitement. Richard McNemar gives this account of the revival at Eagle Creek, the first revival in Ohio:

> *The next camp-meeting was at Eagle Creek, Adams county, Ohio. It began June 5, and continued four days and three nights. The number of people there was not so great, as the county was new; but the work was equally powerful according to the number. At this meeting the principal leading characters in that place fully embraced the spirit of the work, which laid a permanent foundation for its continuance and spread, in that quarter.[1]*

John Dunlavy from Virginia was the Presbyterian minister for a widely scattered congregation.[2] The Transylvania Presbytery of Kentucky held a meeting at Cabin Creek April 1, 1798, and appointed Dunlavy to care for the Congregation of Gilboa, consisting of the settlements at Eagle Creek, Straight Creek, and Red Oak Church.[3] Born in Virginia in 1769, Dunlavy (often spelled Dunlevy) later became part of the Washington Presbytery, the organizing force of the Presbyterian churches north of the Ohio River.

He was the first appointed minister at Red Oak Presbyterian Church from 1800 to 1803. Formed in 1798, Red Oak Church was the first church established in Brown County. It is not the lovely stone building one now finds on Cemetery Road east of Route 68, just south of its juncture with Route 62. The original log church was located about 300 yards from the present building. An 1883 county history relates that "Dunlavy resided on what is now the R. Monnon place, about a mile southwest from Red Oak Presbyterian Church early in the present century."[4] (That location is the present Bealer Road.) When the Springfield Presbytery was formed, some of Dunlavy's congregation became dissatisfied with his preaching "false doctrines." He was forbidden use of the church by the congregation. He ignored the prohibition, "but at the second meeting afterward was met at the door by. . .the sexton, who denied him admission."[5]

To understand the location of the various Eagle Creek and Straight Creek congregations, please be aware that until 1818 Adams and Clermont

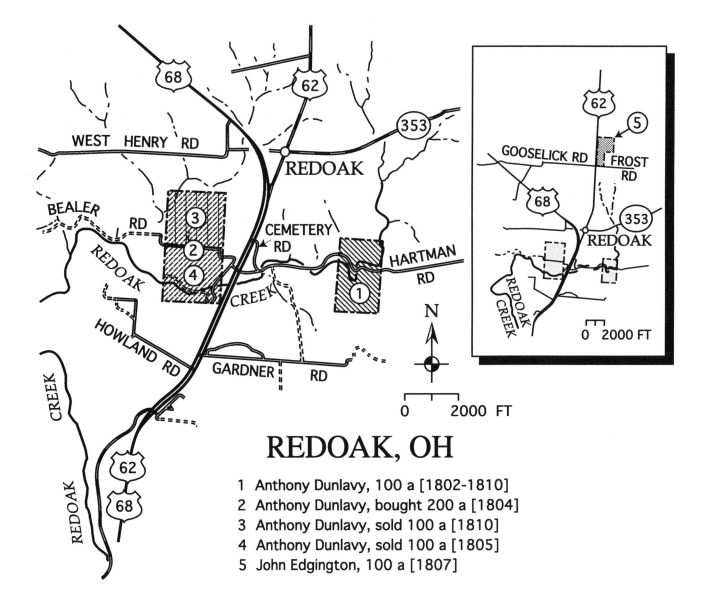

REDOAK, OH

1 Anthony Dunlavy, 100 a [1802-1810]
2 Anthony Dunlavy, bought 200 a [1804]
3 Anthony Dunlavy, sold 100 a [1810]
4 Anthony Dunlavy, sold 100 a [1805]
5 John Edgington, 100 a [1807]

Counties encompassed what are now the eastern and western sections, respectively, of Brown County. Most of the groups whom the Shakers visited and tried to organize into a viable community were located in Brown County. The only reference to a congregation in present Adams County tells about John Dunlavy's church located there:

> *The oldest church organization in West Union [the county seat] is the Presbyterian. This church was formerly organized on East Fork of Eagle Creek by Rev. John Dunlevy and Rev. Richard McNemar about the year 1800. The great Shaker revival in Kentucky had its effect here, and finally resulted in the expulsion of Dunlevy from the Eagle Creek Congregation, whereupon he joined the Shakers. . . .*[6]

This church may well have been located near the Kirker Cemetery and the Kirker Covered Bridge.[7]

When the Shaker missionaries visited the Eagle Creek congregation, Dunlavy was their first convert. At the time he was married to McNemar's sister, Cassia. Benjamin Seth Youngs notes in his journal, "Monday, July 19, 1805 CONFESSION—JOHN DUNLAVY—A Presbyterian Minister afterwards New Light Minister of Eagle Creek Ohio confessed his sins today."[8]

Just a few months before this Shaker conversion, John Dunlavy had purchased land in what is now Byrd Township, Brown County. A cluster of Believers settled nearby including John Knox, William Knox, John Edgington, William Gallagher, Beltshazzar (also spelled Belshazzer, Belteshazer, Belshazzar) Dragoo, and Jonas Painter.

An 1876 county atlas provides this description:

> *Byrd Township is identified with the early religious history of Brown County. The first religion established in the township was that of the Shakers. This religion was preached here as early as 1804 [1805], their first services being held in groves or private houses. Afterwards a structure was erected in which they worshipped, which is described as being "a log pen" of but a few feet in height, and divided into two departments, in one of which the men, and in the other, the women worshipped, which building was afterwards converted into a building more suitable for worship. Their continuance as a religious body was, however, but for a short time, covering a period of only five or six years, when most of them removed elsewhere.*[9]

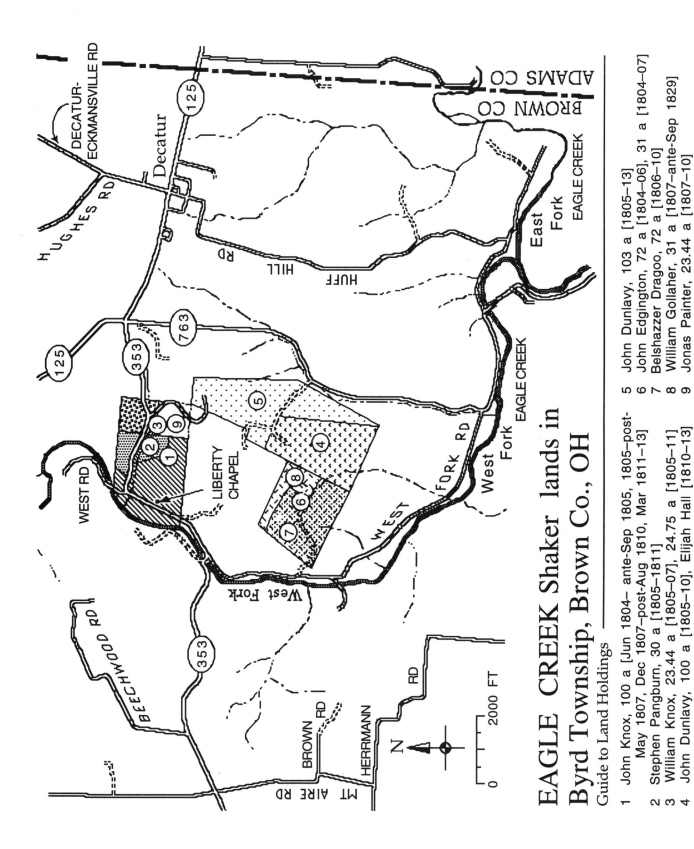

EAGLE CREEK Shaker lands in Byrd Township, Brown Co., OH

Guide to Land Holdings

1 John Knox, 100 a [Jun 1804– ante-Sep 1805, 1805–post–May 1807, Dec 1807–post-Aug 1810, Mar 1811–13]
2 Stephen Pangburn, 30 a [1805–1811]
3 William Knox, 23.44 a [1805–07], 24.75 a [1805–11]
4 John Dunlavy, 100 a [1805–10], Elijah Hall [1810–13]
5 John Dunlavy, 103 a [1805–13]
6 John Edgington, 72 a [1804–06], 31 a [1804–07]
7 Belshazzer Dragoo, 72 a [1806–10]
8 William Gollaher, 31 a [1807–ante-Sep 1829]
9 Jonas Painter, 23.44 a [1807–10]

"At Eagle Creek, met at John Knoxes—about 90 Believers.
Held meeting in a log meeting house."

Youngs adds in his journal, "At Eagle Creek, met at John Knoxes—about 90 Believers. Held meeting in a log meeting house."[10] The description of "a log pen" structure in Byrd Township and the reference by Youngs to a meeting house near Knoxes puts the location of a Shaker meeting house in the Liberty Chapel neighborhood southwest of Decatur.

A fourth location for these Shakers was the Bridgewater neighborhood in Brown County. This area is east of Georgetown along Straight Creek and the town of Bridgewater, which no longer exists today but vied to be the county seat in the early 1800s. There are some diary notations of Shaker visits to John Sharp's in the Bridgewater area. For March 10, 1806, Youngs noted that they "went to Garner McNemar's—thence 8 miles to John Sharp's where we held meeting & spoke about 2 hours to a listening people."[11]

Deeds for John Sharp's land are located in Clermont County records. One acreage was located along White Oak Creek north of Georgetown. His other land along Straight Creek was located close to others mentioned in early records: Elijah Hall, Thomas Vance, and Charles Hall.

These family groups, scattered over such a large land area, never became a cohesive group. Youngs chronicles the visit that he, Elder Issachar Bates, and Richard McNemar made to the Eagle Creek congregation on January 5, 1806:

> At noon we met with the Believers at Jno Knox's—about 30 in number & as many spectators—to whom John Dunlavy, Richard McNemar, Elds. Issachar & Benjn. spoke with a measure of freedom for about 3 hours.
>
> In the evening most of the believers met again & after speaking a long time & singing hymns we went into the worship of God, the first time publicly in this place. It was a profitable time to the people numbers who went forth were very happy—it was a time of power—some fell, others danced, even among those who had not opened their minds—A[nthony] Dunlavy who had never before been exercised, was taken with shaking & jerking—from that to dancing which continued for 4 hours with scarce any intermission.[12]

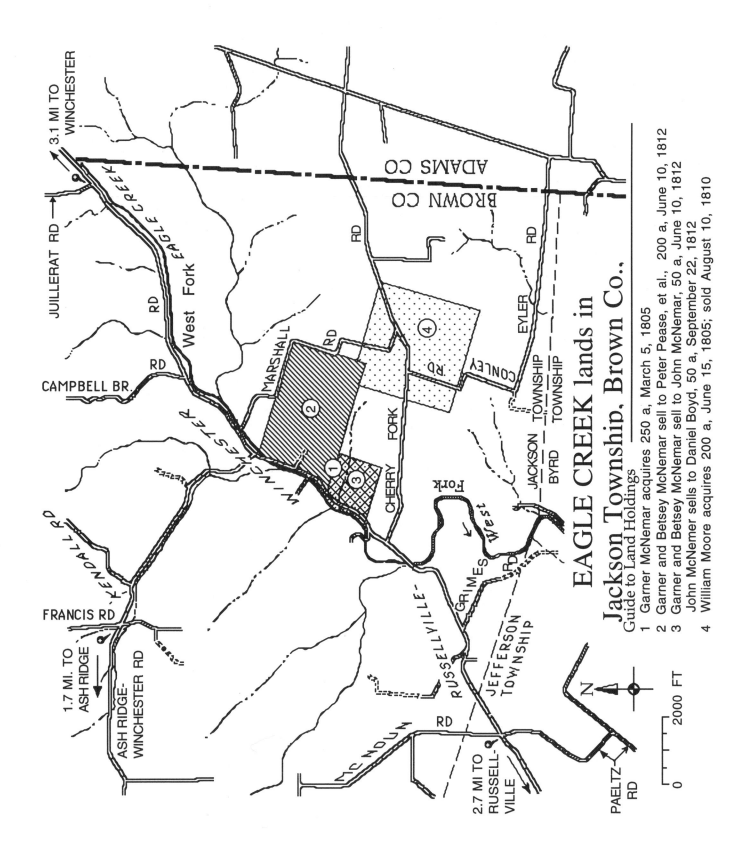

EAGLE CREEK lands in
Jackson Township, Brown Co..
Guide to Land Holdings

1 Garner McNemar acquires 250 a, March 5, 1805
2 Garner and Betsey McNemar sell to Peter Pease, et al., 200 a, June 10, 1812
3 Garner and Betsey McNemar sell to John McNemar, 50 a, June 10, 1812
  John McNemar sells to Daniel Boyd, 50 a, September 22, 1812
4 William Moore acquires 200 a, June 15, 1805; sold August 10, 1810

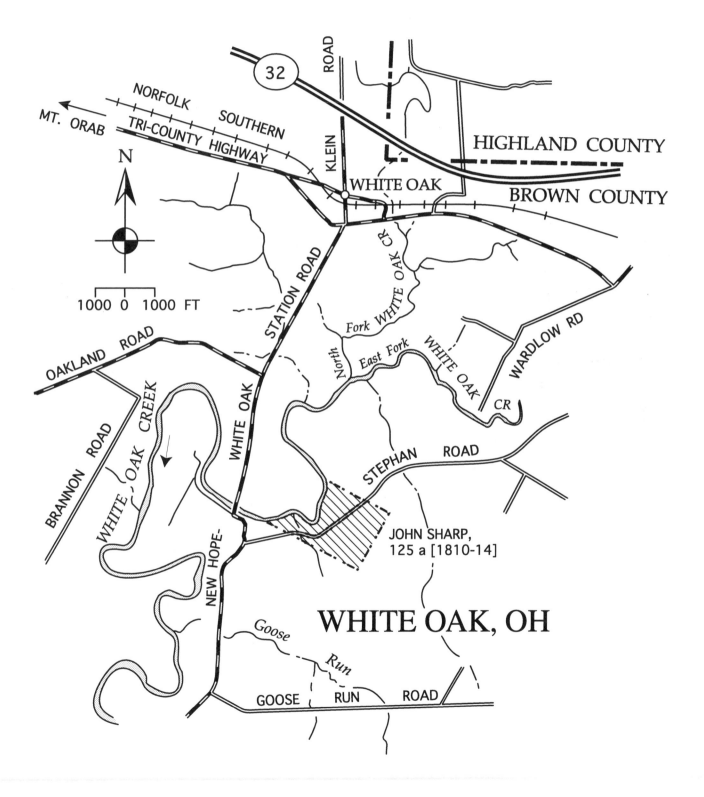

WHITE OAK, OH

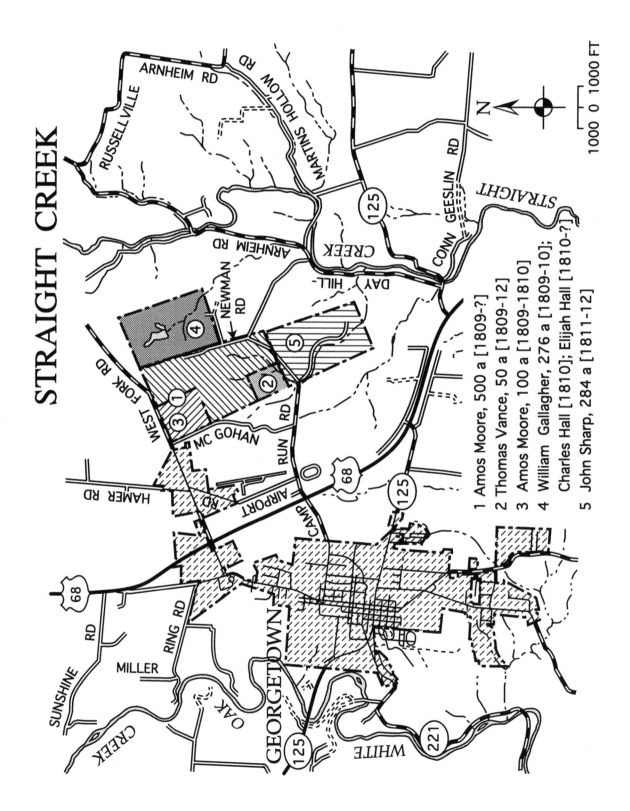

STRAIGHT CREEK

1 Amos Moore, 500 a [1809-?]
2 Thomas Vance, 50 a [1809-12]
3 Amos Moore, 100 a [1809-1810]
4 William Gallagher, 276 a [1809-10];
  Charles Hall [1810]; Elijah Hall [1810-?]
5 John Sharp, 284 a [1811-12]

"It is most evident that the people have run thro & are at a full stop in this place..."

Although there were frequent visits from Union Village with the Eagle Creek and Straight Creek Believers, there were often reports of backsliding. On Sunday, August 31, 1806, Youngs noted:

At Eagle Creek, Ohio—At noon to day the believers met, & about 80 or 100 spectators, Issachar & Benj. spoke about 2 hours—had an intermission—Jno. Davis & Issachar spoke again—after which we went forth in the Dance—but for months past the wicked had great power here—believers running wild with gifts & going to destruction—John Edgington sang with the brethren—He & his wife were among the first who believed here—had fallen back a year—but returned & reunited last Sabbath.[13]

By February 1810 the problems still festered. On the 6th, Youngs wrote: "Went to John Knoxs attended meeting, spoke again of their scattered & selfish & discouraging condition—to prepare them for coming together." The very next day it was noted, "PURCHASING LANDS— Full liberty was given to Brn. George Legier & Wm. Gallagher to purchase 1000 acres of land, half way between Eagle & strait creeks."[14] There is no record of any such land transaction in either Adams County or Clermont County.

After two more visits from Union Village, Elder Benjamin sums up the matter: "It is most evident that the people have run thro & are at a full stop in this place—and also that their general & particular feelings are to be up & gone out of it. After a trial of about 5 years (!) every endeavor to find an opening for a foundation has failed."[15]

In May and June of 1810, there were further visits from Union Village to Eagle Creek suggesting "their removal to Busroe." By March 1811, 80 souls moved by land or by river to Busro or West Union, another Shaker community taking shape on the Indiana frontier. Seventy moved to Union Village, making 150 persons from that part of Ohio.

Dunlavy relocated at Pleasant Hill, Kentucky, where his noteworthy Shaker theology, *The Manifesto, or a Declaration of the Doctrines and Practice of the Church of Christ*, was published in 1818. He died at West Union in 1826.

MT REPOSE, OH

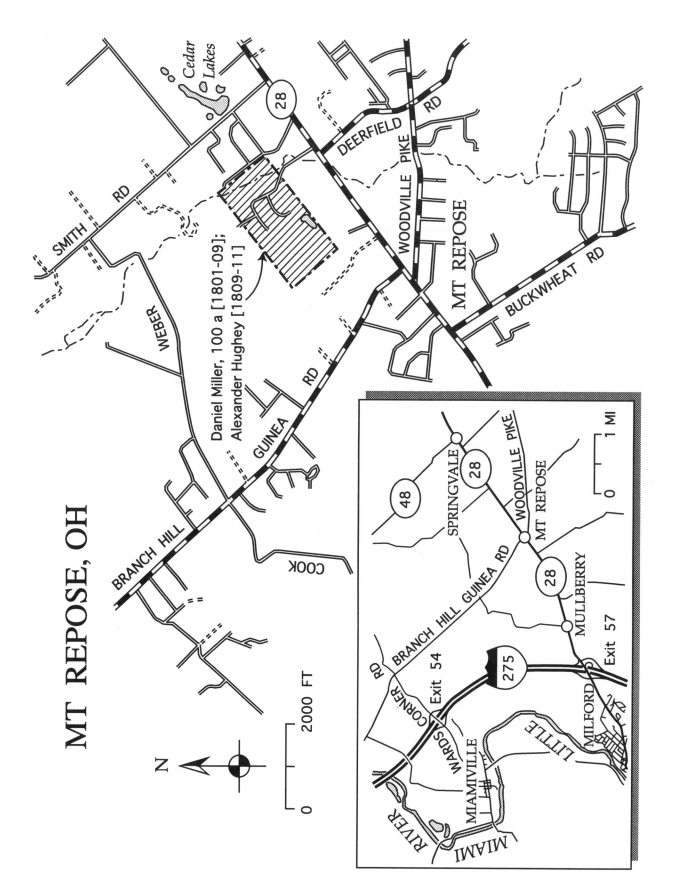

Cedar Lakes

28

DEERFIELD RD

WOODVILLE PIKE

MT REPOSE

BUCKWHEAT RD

SMITH RD

WEBER

Daniel Miller, 100 a [1801-09]; Alexander Hughey [1809-11]

GUINEA RD

BRANCH HILL

COOK

N

2000 FT

0

SPRINGVALE

48

28

WOODVILLE PIKE

MT REPOSE

28

MULLBERRY

BRANCH HILL GUINEA RD

WARDS CORNER RD

Exit 54

275

Exit 57

MIAMIVILLE

MILFORD

LITTLE

MIAMI RIVER

0   1 MI

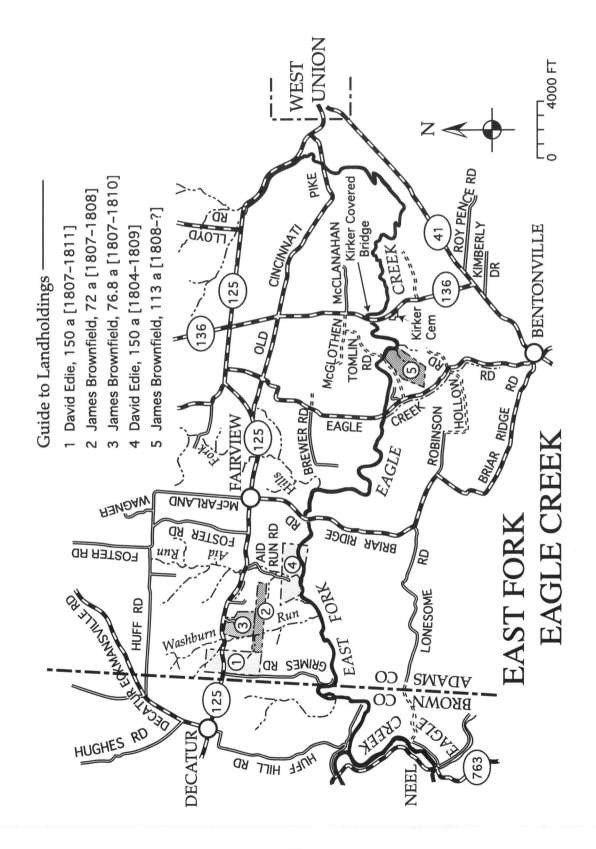

Guide to Landholdings ───

1 David Edie, 150 a [1807–1811]
2 James Brownfield, 72 a [1807–1808]
3 James Brownfield, 76.8 a [1807–1810]
4 David Edie, 150 a [1804–1809]
5 James Brownfield, 113 a [1808–?]

EAST FORK
EAGLE CREEK

4000 FT

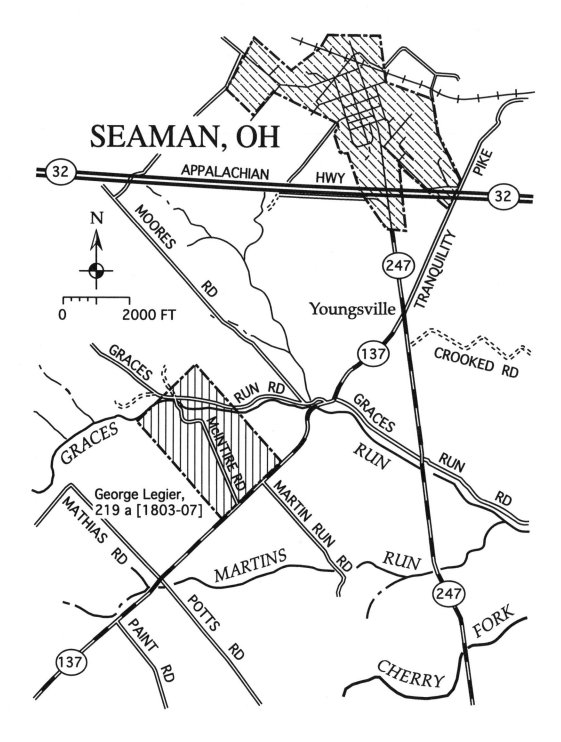

SEAMAN, OH

32 APPALACHIAN HWY 32

N

0 2000 FT

MOORES RD

247

TRANQUILITY PIKE

Youngsville

137

CROOKED RD

GRACES RUN RD

McINTIRE RD

GRACES

GRACES RUN RUN RD

George Legier,
219 a [1803-07]

MATHIAS RD

MARTIN RUN RD

MARTINS RUN

247

137

PAINT RD

POTTS RD

CHERRY FORK

RIPLEY, OH

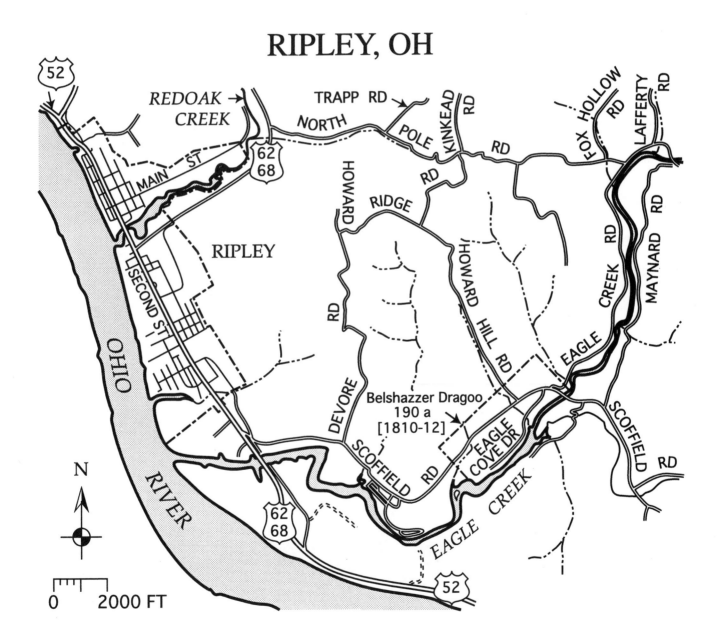

52

REDOAK CREEK

TRAPP RD

NORTH

POLE RD

KINKEAD RD

RD

FOX HOLLOW RD

LAFFERTY RD

62 68

MAIN ST

HOWARD RIDGE RD

RIPLEY

HOWARD HILL RD

EAGLE CREEK RD

MAYNARD RD

SECOND ST

OHIO RIVER

DEVORE RD

Belshazzer Dragoo
190 a
[1810-12]

EAGLE COVE DR

SCOFFIELD RD

EAGLE

SCOFFIELD RD

N

62 68

EAGLE CREEK

52

0   2000 FT

RATTLESNAKE CREEK

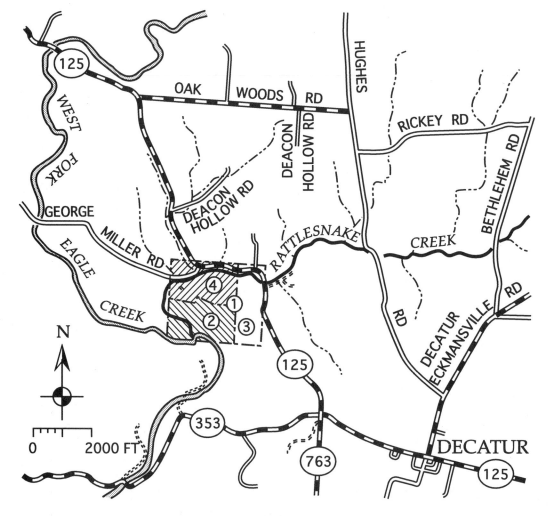

1 John Johnson, acquired 202.25 a [1807]
2 John Johnson, sold 70 a [1807]
   Joseph Johnson, 70 a [1807–10]
3 John Johnson, sold 62 a [1808]
4 John Johnson, sold 70 a [1810]

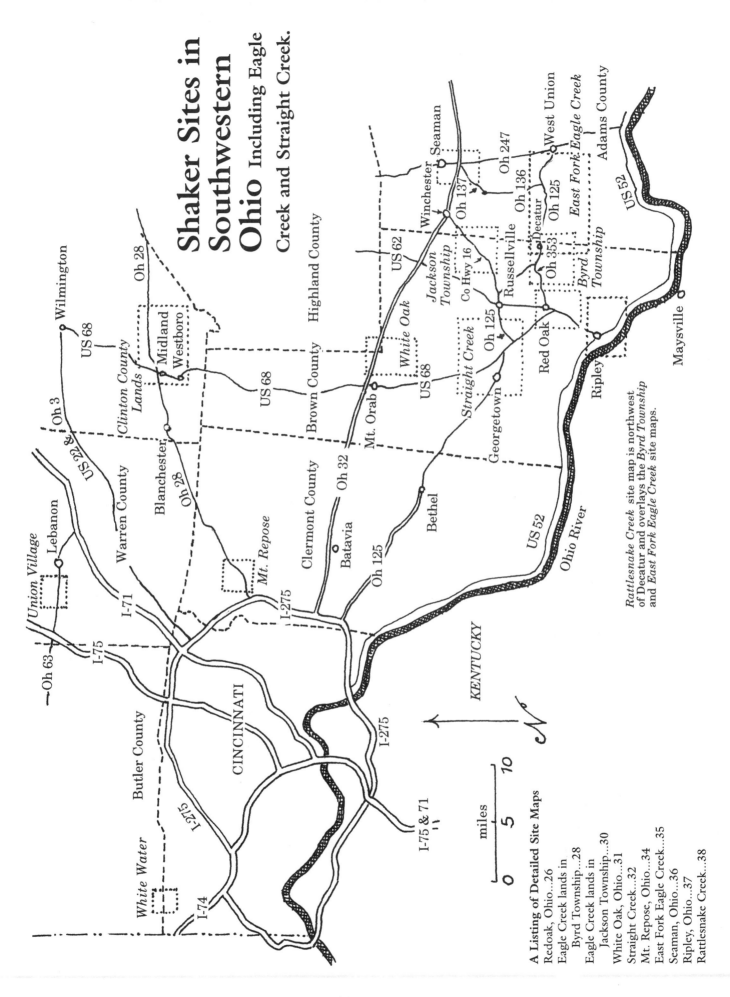

Shaker Sites in Southwestern Ohio Including Eagle Creek and Straight Creek.

Rattlesnake Creek site map is northwest of Decatur and overlays the *Byrd Township* and *East Fork Eagle Creek* site maps.

A Listing of Detailed Site Maps

Redoak, Ohio...26
Eagle Creek lands in Byrd Township...28
Eagle Creek lands in Jackson Township...30
White Oak, Ohio...31
Straight Creek...32
Mt. Repose, Ohio...34
East Fork Eagle Creek...35
Seaman, Ohio...36
Ripley, Ohio...37
Rattlesnake Creek...38

KENTUCKY

N

miles
0 5 10

Adams County

Highland County

Brown County

Clermont County

Warren County

Butler County

Clinton County Lands

Byrd Township

Jackson Township

White Oak

Straight Creek

East Fork Eagle Creek

Wilmington
US 68
Oh 28
Midland
Westboro
Oh 3
US 22 & 3
Oh 28
Blanchester
Oh 28
US 68
US 68
Union Village
Lebanon
Oh 63
I-75
I-71
I-275
Mt. Repose
I-275
I-275
White Water
I-74
I-75 & 71
CINCINNATI
I-275
Bethel
Batavia
Oh 125
Oh 32
Mt. Orab
US 68
Georgetown
Red Oak
Oh 125
Oh 125
Russellville
Co Hwy 16
US 62
Winchester
Seaman
Oh 137
Oh 247
Decatur
Oh 136
Oh 353
Oh 125
West Union
US 52
Maysville
Ripley
US 52
Ohio River
East Fork Eagle Creek

[1] McNemar, *Kentucky Revival*, 25.

[2] Carl N. Thompson, Compiler, *Historical Collections of Brown County, Ohio* (Piqua, Ohio: Hammer Graphics, 1969), 1006, gives this bit of Dunlavy genealogy: "The Dunlevy family had migrated to Ireland from France about 1680. . . . Originally, they were not French, but Hugenot Spaniards, and they were compelled to leave France on account of the persecutions in 1650. The name was originally Don Levi, but changed later to read Dunlevy."

[3] Byron Williams, *History of Clermont and Brown Counties, Ohio* (Milford, Ohio: Hobart Publishing Co., 1913), 358.

[4] W. H. Beers, *History of Brown County, Ohio* (Chicago: W. H. Beers & Co., 1883), 413-414.

[5] Ibid., 414.

[6] Nelson W. Evans and Emmons B. Stivers, *History of Adams County* (West Union, Ohio: E.B. Stivers, 1900), 477.

[7] In the Shaker file at the Brown County Genealogical Society Museum in Georgetown is the notation of four Shaker sites in that part of Ohio: The Kirker Cemetery Neighborhood on East fork of Eagle Creek southwest of West Union; The Red Oak Neighborhood; the Liberty Chapel Neighborhood southwest of Decatur, and the "Bridgewater" Neighborhood on Straight Creek south of Arnheim.

[8] *South Union Record A*, 44.

[9] D.J. Lake and B.N. Griffing, *Atlas of Brown County, Ohio* (Philadelphia: Lake, Griffing & Stevenson Co., 1876), 26.

[10] *Record A*, April 25, 1809, 100.

[11] Ibid., 57.

[12] Ibid., 49.

[13] Ibid., 69.

[14] Ibid., 117.

[15] Ibid.

Chapter 9

Watervliet

Montgomery and Greene Counties, Ohio

The fiery spirit of the camp meetings reached 22 miles north of Union Village to a community of Scotch Presbyterian families, primarily from Kentucky. In Ohio this group settled along the waters of the Beaver Creek, six miles southeast of Dayton.

When the three missionaries from New Lebanon established Union Village near Lebanon in 1805, they organized a camp meeting at that location, attracting a huge crowd. Most of the congregation at Beaver Creek,

Watervliet - Ohio   David L. Smith

Watervliet Center Family Dwelling

members of Beulah Church, attended the meeting. Swept up in the passion of the camp meeting, William Stewart invited the Shakers from Union Village to visit the Beaver Creek community. Two revivals were then held at Beulah, one at the end of May, the other June 22. John Huston, a wheelwright and farmer, became the first convert.

There were visits back and forth between Union Village and the Beulah congregation. By April 1806 there were about a dozen Believers, including John Patterson, the first settler in the area in 1799. His property formed the nucleus for the village along Beaver Creek. When Issachar Bates and Benjamin Seth Youngs visited them and brought them all together on

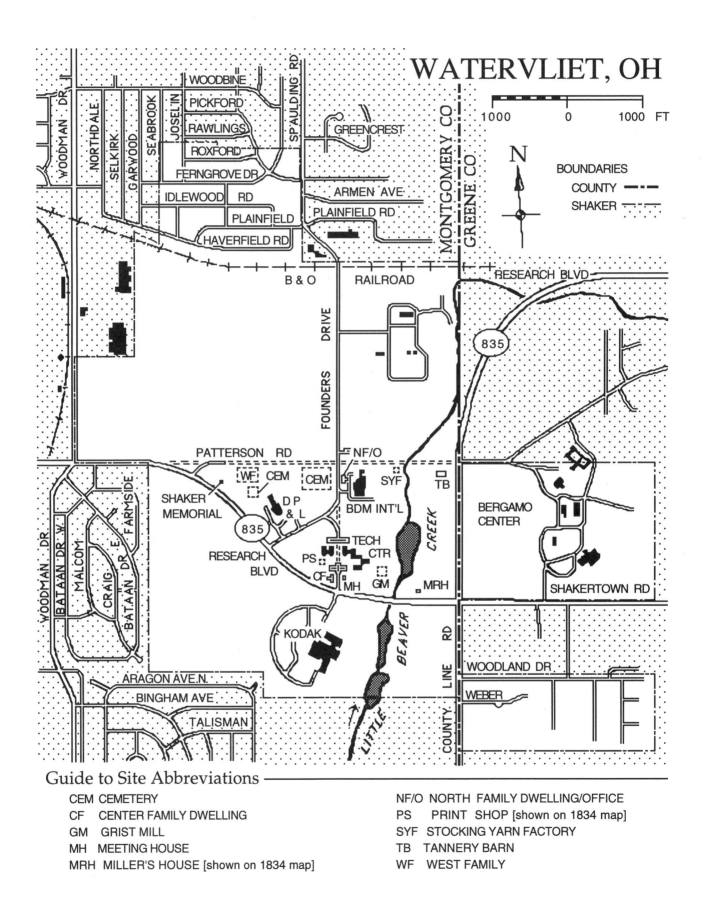

WATERVLIET, OH

1000　0　1000 FT

BOUNDARIES
COUNTY ━ ‒ ━ ‒
SHAKER ‒‒‒‒‒‒

Guide to Site Abbreviations

CEM CEMETERY
CF CENTER FAMILY DWELLING
GM GRIST MILL
MH MEETING HOUSE
MRH MILLER'S HOUSE [shown on 1834 map]

NF/O NORTH FAMILY DWELLING/OFFICE
PS PRINT SHOP [shown on 1834 map]
SYF STOCKING YARN FACTORY
TB TANNERY BARN
WF WEST FAMILY

April 26, 1806, it was recorded that "all met together and went forth to worship in the dance."[1] That is considered the founding date for this second Shaker community established in the West.

Issachar Bates, one of the Shaker missionaries from New Lebanon, was later an elder for this emerging community. It was not until 1813 that a Union Village journal referred to the community as Water Vliet. The name Watervliet was assumed by the group to honor the first Shaker settlement. Over the years the community grew to 643 acres in Montgomery County and 160 acres in adjacent Greene County.

During the early 1830s Richard McNemar came from Union Village as elder for Watervliet. A print shop was organized and extensive Shaker printing was produced at Watervliet by McNemar. Among his publications was a hymn book with a blue paper cover. He had the habit of putting together printed material in various sequences so that the page numbers did not always run true. It has left scholars comparing notes to this day.

It was under the direction of Richard Pelham in the 1840s that the woolen mill was established, producing a good income for the community. Moses Eastwood went on peddling trips selling stocking yarn when he was not tending his orchards and gardens.

Watervliet was never a large community. In 1856, 20 members from White Water came to strengthen the membership. When North Union closed in 1889, Clymena Miner brought 12 brethren and eight other sisters to Watervliet. The community had about 100 members at its height. After the Civil War its membership suffered a steady decline. Because of the mounting debts at Union Village, Elder Joseph Slingerland abruptly closed Watervliet in the fall of 1900. Members went to live at Union Village.

In the early twentieth century the lands of Watervliet became a farm for a nearby mental health facility and was known as the State Farm. In 1981 the state turned the property over to a foundation which created a research park.

The landscape of the Miami Valley Research Park and the Bergamo Retreat Center, as well as rows of homes, make it difficult to visualize the Watervliet Shaker community. Beaver Creek has been slightly moved and a lake created, belying the location of grist mills and the woolen mill.

A miller's house and a tannery barn have been moved from this site to the Kettering-Moraine Museum at 35 Moraine Circle South, Kettering,

...two buildings at the Kettering-Moraine Museum are the only Shaker buildings open to the public in Ohio.

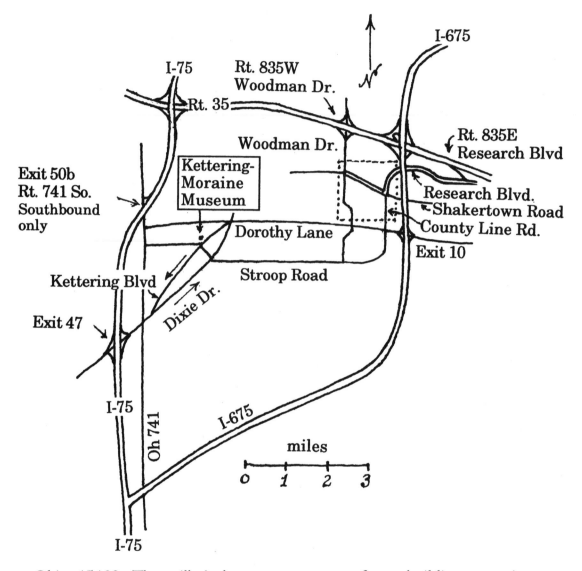

Ohio 45439. The miller's house, a two-story frame building, contains a collection of Shaker artifacts. Early in 1996, the 33 by 64-foot, post-and-beam tannery barn was reconstructed by Amish woodworkers at the museum. These two buildings at the Kettering-Moraine Museum are the only Shaker buildings open to the public in Ohio. The museum is open Sunday afternoons from 1 P.M. to 5 P.M., or by appointment with the director, Mrs. Melba Hunt, (937) 299-2722.

---

[1] *South Union Record A*, 61.

Chapter 10

Pleasant Hill

Mercer County, Kentucky

*Pleasant Hill Trustees' Office
Ministry's Shop and Meeting House*

As the three missionaries from New Lebanon, whom J.P. MacLean called "the Shaker propaganda," criss-crossed Ohio, Indiana, and Kentucky, they often visited Shawnee Run in Mercer County, Kentucky. Benjamin Seth Youngs chronicled their first visit:

> *Elisha Thomas, Saml. & Henry Bonta, from Mercer County with others were determined to hear [the missionaries] speak—drew them to a private house for the purpose & when they heard the testimony from Benjn. received faith & shortly after Elisha Saml. & Henry opened their minds, which was the beginning of the gospel being planted in Mercer Co. Ky.[1]*

Hundreds of spectators were attracted to the Bontas' and Elisha Thomas' barns for worship when the missionaries appeared. Youngs reported on June 1, 1806: "Meeting at Elisha Thomas' Barn—400 spectators. Benj. addressed them—Believers had worship in songs & dances—kneeling etc."[2] It was Elisha Thomas' 140-acre farm which became the nucleus for the Pleasant Hill community. The first covenant with the Shakers was accepted there in December 1806.

The early Kentucky Shakers chose this site of Pleasant Hill for its agricultural potential and proximity to the Kentucky River. Both features contributed to the success of the community, which by 1820 included more than 4,000 acres of fertile land and 500 industrious inhabitants. As the village flourished, it grew to five families: Centre, East, West, West Lot, and North Lot, along with nearby mill sites.

Primarily an agricultural community, their livestock, garden seeds, herbs, and other products were marketed as far away as New Orleans. The

8

It was Elisha Thomas' 140-acre farm which became the nucleus for the Pleasant Hill community.

Shakers also produced tinware, woodenware, brooms, and textiles for their own use and for sale.

Considered the master architect of many of the Pleasant Hill buildings, Micajah Burnett was sometimes called "The Thomas Jefferson of the West." He came to the Society with his parents in 1809 and was responsible for the basic plan of the village. The 1820 Meeting House is adjudged by many as the most ingeniously designed and constructed building at Pleasant Hill. To create a space free of central obstructions for the Shakers' worship services, his plan included the support of the entire overhead structure with heavy trusses beneath the roof. This masterful design, similar to that of a covered bridge, provides both strength and stability. Another example of structural suspension along with a coupling of function and beauty is the twin spiral staircases connecting the three floors of the Trustees' Office, truly a tribute to the genius of Micajah Burnett.

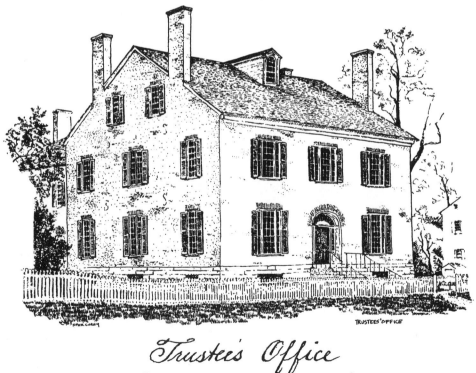

*Trustee's Office
Pleasant Hill, Ky.*

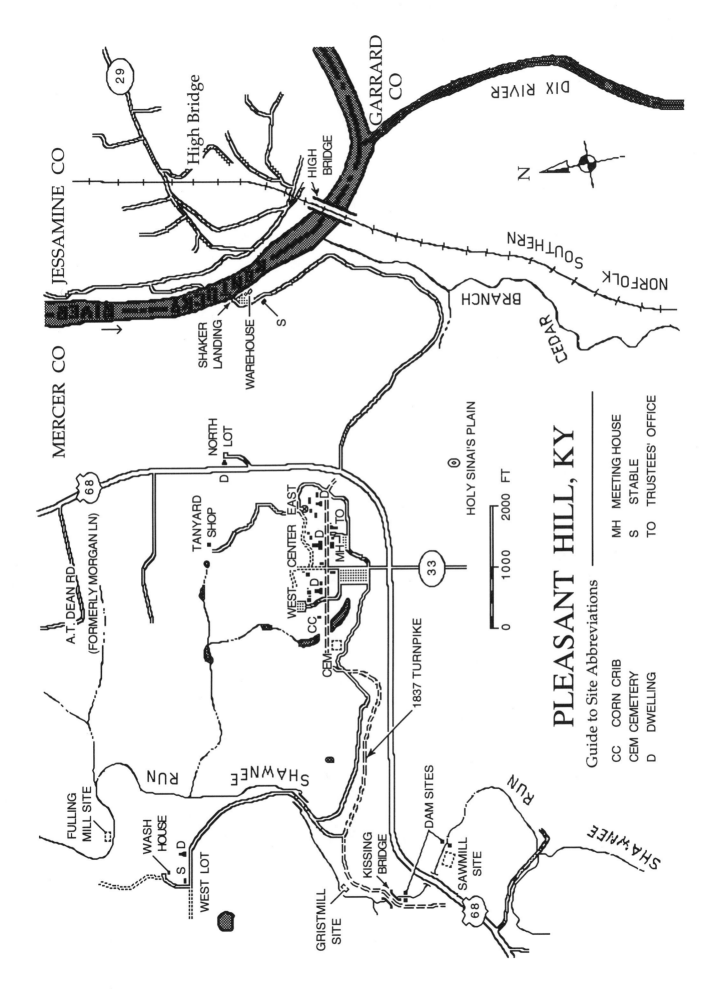

PLEASANT HILL, KY

Guide to Site Abbreviations

CC CORN CRIB
CEM CEMETERY
D DWELLING

MH MEETING HOUSE
S STABLE
TO TRUSTEES' OFFICE

MERCER CO

JESSAMINE CO

GARRARD CO

High Bridge

HIGH BRIDGE

DIX RIVER

KENTUCKY RIVER

SHAKER LANDING

WAREHOUSE S

NORFOLK SOUTHERN

CEDAR BRANCH

A.T. DEAN RD.
(FORMERLY MORGAN LN)

TANYARD SHOP

NORTH LOT D

WEST- CENTER EAST

CC CEM

MH TO

HOLY SINAI'S PLAIN

2000 FT
1000
0

1837 TURNPIKE

FULLING MILL SITE

WASH HOUSE S D

WEST LOT

SHAWNEE RUN

GRISTMILL SITE

KISSING BRIDGE

DAM SITES

SAWMILL SITE

SHAWNEE RUN

N

47

The Civil War years were devastating for the two Kentucky communities. Their journals reflect the hardships they endured. Although their pacifism was generally respected by both the North and South, Federal and Confederate troops were fed as they passed and re-passed through the village. Such services depleted the Shakers' food supplies along with their stock of horses and wagons. Their trade came to a standstill, with dire results to their economy.

The Civil War, industrialization, and other changes in society all contributed to the decline of Pleasant Hill. The village closed in 1910. An agreement was made with George Bohon, a Harrodsburg banker, to care for the remaining 12 aged Shakers. The last Shaker, Sister Mary Settles, died in the village in 1923.

The present restoration began in 1961 under the leadership of two dedicated Kentuckians, Earl D. Wallace, whose expertise and vision involved fund raising, and James Lowry Cogar, the first curator of Colonial Williamsburg, who supervised the restoration. Pleasant Hill is now an "Historic Museum Village" and a model for historic preservation. It is a National Historic Landmark, the first in the United States to be so designated from boundary to boundary. Thirty-three original buildings have been restored, and an operating farm of 2,700 acres surrounds the village, providing a safe insulative zone just as it did when the Shakers owned it.

All visitor services are provided in original buildings, including overnight accommodations, outstanding meals, and interpretation of Shaker life and crafts. Original Shaker furniture and other items are exhibited in the 40-room Centre Family Dwelling. Shaker music is presented in the Meeting House. Educational programs are offered, and there are year-round special events and workshops. Seasonal interpretive trips are scheduled on the Kentucky River aboard the sternwheeler *Dixie Belle*. Archeological studies and research are ongoing to expand knowledge of the community's early history. Highway 68 has been rerouted around the community, allowing the old turnpike from Shawnee Run through the center of the village to recapture its 1840 appearance.

Today visitors can truly experience the spirit of the Shakers and their quest for simplicity and perfection in the legacy of Pleasant Hill.

Jean Dones

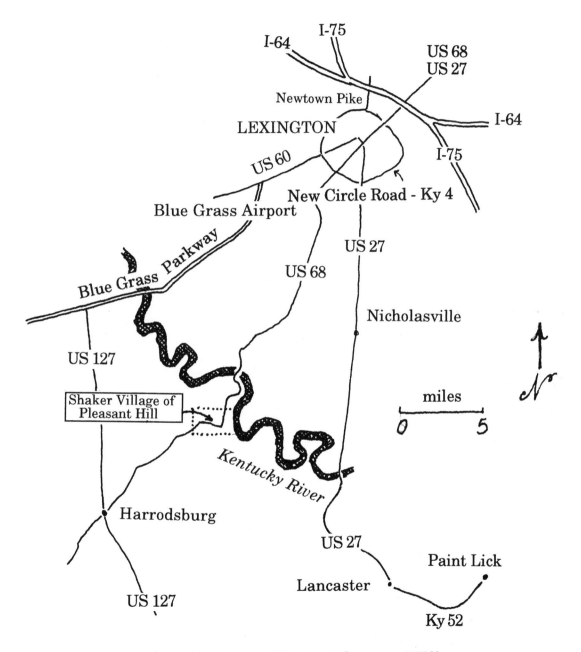

Planning Your Visit to Pleasant Hill

The Shaker Village at Pleasant Hill lives up to its motto, "We make you kindly welcome." In addition to memorable dining in the Trustees' Building and overnight accommodations in the original Shaker buildings, special programs are planned for almost every weekend. Village nature walks are available in the spring and fall. The Pleasant Hill Singers provide special

*Ministry's Workshop
Pleasant Hill, Ky.*

musical weekends with performances in the 1820 Meeting House. Silk culturing, tinsmithing, herb demonstrations, blacksmithing, woodworking, and apple cider pressing all come alive at Pleasant Hill. Call (606) 734-5411 for a calendar of events. Or write to Shaker Village of Pleasant Hill, 3501 Lexington Road, Harrodsburg, Kentucky 40330. Special room rates are available for January through March.

The Shaker Village riverboat, Dixie Belle, offers one-hour excursions to enjoy the scenic Kentucky River Palisades from the last Friday in April through October 31. Excursion times: 10 A.M., NOON, 2, 4, and 6 P.M.

[1] *South Union Record A*, end of June, 1805, 45.

[2] Ibid., 48.

Chapter 11

South Union

Logan, Simpson, and Warren Counties, Kentucky

Following on the heels of the great Kentucky revival, Issachar Bates, Richard McNemar, and Matthew Houston journeyed to the Gasper River area of Logan County, Kentucky, in October 1807. Their intense missionary work bore fruit, and within a month they heard confessions from John and Jesse McComb, Neal Patterson, Presbyterian minister John Rankin, Charles and Sally Eads, and more than 20 others.[1]

Jesse McComb's brick house was the first building occupied by the Gasper Believers. Rankin's house became the dwelling of the East Family. In 1811 the Central Ministry at New Lebanon, New York, appointed four eastern Shakers—Benjamin Seth Youngs, Joseph Allen, Molly Goodrich, and Mercy Pickett—as spiritual leaders at Gasper. Within a few years the community became known as South Union.[2]

South Union grew rapidly, eventually acquiring 6,000 acres of land including an outfamily[3] at Black Lick and a mill family at Drakes Creek. Over 250 buildings were erected. The sale of packaged garden seeds, flour, meal, canned and preserved fruit, hats, palm-leaf bonnets, and brooms sustained the South Union Shakers for many years. Their livestock sales included pure-bred hogs and shorthorn cattle.

South Union numbered nearly 300 members by 1814[4] and peaked at approximately 350 in 1827 when 31 individuals arrived after the abandonment of West Union. Although membership fluctuated and even dipped below 200 late in the 1830s and early 1840s, it typically ranged from 240 to 250 in the midyears of the nineteenth century.[5]

A View of South Union

N

ALBSpence

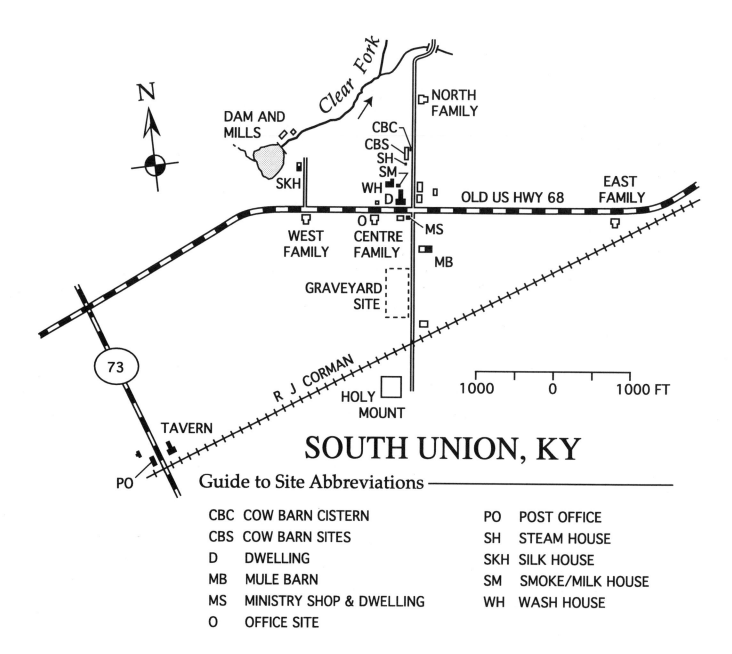

SOUTH UNION, KY

Guide to Site Abbreviations

CBC	COW BARN CISTERN		PO	POST OFFICE
CBS	COW BARN SITES		SH	STEAM HOUSE
D	DWELLING		SKH	SILK HOUSE
MB	MULE BARN		SM	SMOKE/MILK HOUSE
MS	MINISTRY SHOP & DWELLING		WH	WASH HOUSE
O	OFFICE SITE			

*South Union grew rapidly, eventually acquiring
6,000 acres of land including an outfamily
at Black Lick and a mill family at Drakes Creek.*

Centre House at South Union, Ky.

Because of its geographical location, the Civil War had a greater impact on life and commerce at South Union than perhaps any other Shaker community.[6] Just west of the main village lay a major north-south route to the lower reaches of the Green River that were navigable by steamboats from the Ohio River. On east-west axes were a state highway linking forts at Bowling Green to Russellville, where a provisional Confederate Government of Kentucky was formed, and the Memphis branch of the Louisville and Nashville Railroad.

The railroad became a focus of skirmishes. Wave upon wave of Federal and Confederate troops crying for meals decimated Shaker crops and pantries. Agents commandeered Shaker horses, wagons, and blanket cloth. During the war the Shakers' Depot burned and business opportunities stagnated.[7]

Two years after the conflict, membership at South Union rose to 301. Amazingly by 1874, South Union achieved numerical parity with Union Village and Pleasant Hill, communities which had always known much larger memberships.[8] Eventually, however, forces of decline took hold.

The community dropped to 55 members by 1900.[9] When South Union disbanded in 1922, only nine Shakers were left. Sister Josie Bridges and Elder Logan Johns were taken to the East. The other seven received settlements of $10,000 apiece.[10] The demise of the community at South Union ended Western Shakerism after 117 years.

Significant buildings maintain the Shaker imprint on the area. In 1822 the brethren began excavating the cellar and cutting foundation stones for the 40-room 1824 Centre House. The dwelling stresses the symmetrical elements of Georgian architecture. Inside are classic Shaker double doors and staircases, multi-drawered built-in cabinets, and the ever present peg strips along the walls

The current Shaker Museum, located in the Centre House, is filled with a fine collection of original South Union artifacts. Baskets, silk and linen pieces, tools, and manuscripts as well as trestle tables, chairs, and other furnishings display the exemplary Shaker craftsmanship and material culture found at South Union. The museum also houses the Julia Neal Library with its wide assortment of primary and secondary South Union materials.

Of the nine remaining structures at South Union, the Museum currently owns five, including the Shaker Tavern. Built by the Shakers in 1869 in an attempt to recoup losses incurred by the Civil War, the Shaker Tavern operates today as a bed and breakfast. The nearby 1917 Shaker Store serves as South Union's post office.

The 1835 Smoke and Milk House as well as the 1847 brick Steam House, located behind the Centre House, have undergone restoration in recent years.

The 1854 Wash House is adjacent to the Shaker Museum and is owned by the Fathers of Mercy Catholic Order. Constructed for the women in the Shaker village, the Wash House has the unique feature of three doors in its south facade.

The Ministry's Shop, built in 1846, is directly across the road from the Shaker Museum. It serves as a private residence.

The Shaker Museum continues further development of the South Union historic site in areas such as original land and building acquisition and interpretation, educational programming and research.

Mike Sisk and Dale Covington

The demise of the community at South Union ended Western Shakerism after 117 years.

Black Lick or Watervliet
Logan County, Kentucky

Black Lick, widely recognized as the most fertile land in Logan County, was located four miles west of South Union. The soil around the springs contained salt and sulfur that attracted herds of deer and buffalo. Not far from the springs that fed Black Lick Creek passed the major overland route connecting Bowling Green and Russellville in the early days of the nineteenth century.

At summer's end in 1812, 47 of nearly 300 Believers from the temporarily vacated community at Busro remained at South Union, substantially swelling the membership of this Kentucky community. South Union trustees began negotiating to purchase 1,140 acres at Black Lick for $8 an acre, and the sale was completed in January 1813.[11] Shaker brethren quickly built a sugar camp and sowed 18 acres of flax.

A family order was established at Black Lick on November 29, 1813, built around seven Believers from South Union led by Francis Whyte and Rebecca Davis.[12] By April 1814 there were 44 residents. Sarah Lowery became Eldress in 1815 and stood for years with Francis Whyte in the Elders' order at Black Lick. By 1816 Black Lick became the home for South Union's children.

Farm improvements continued. An orchard was planted, corn and hay were gathered, and a dwelling house was constructed. An 1836 map of the farm shows, in addition to the dwelling house and orchard, a meat house, barn, shop, meadow, pastures, and grain fields. In 1822 the farm was renamed Watervliet after the New York Shaker home of Mother Ann Lee and where South Union's beloved leader, Benjamin Seth Youngs, had his Shaker roots.

Notwithstanding these strong beginnings, Isaac Newton Youngs and Elder Rufus Bishop (Elder Rufus stood second in the Central Ministry at New Lebanon, New York) on a tour of Ohio and Kentucky in 1834, found only 18 Believers in this, "the very remotest corner of the gospel vineyard." The family was broken up in union with all concerned in 1837.[13] However, the Shakers continued to own at least part of the farm until 1885.

The Shakers sold two tracts at Watervliet that were significant in the economic development of the area. In September 1838 trustees George

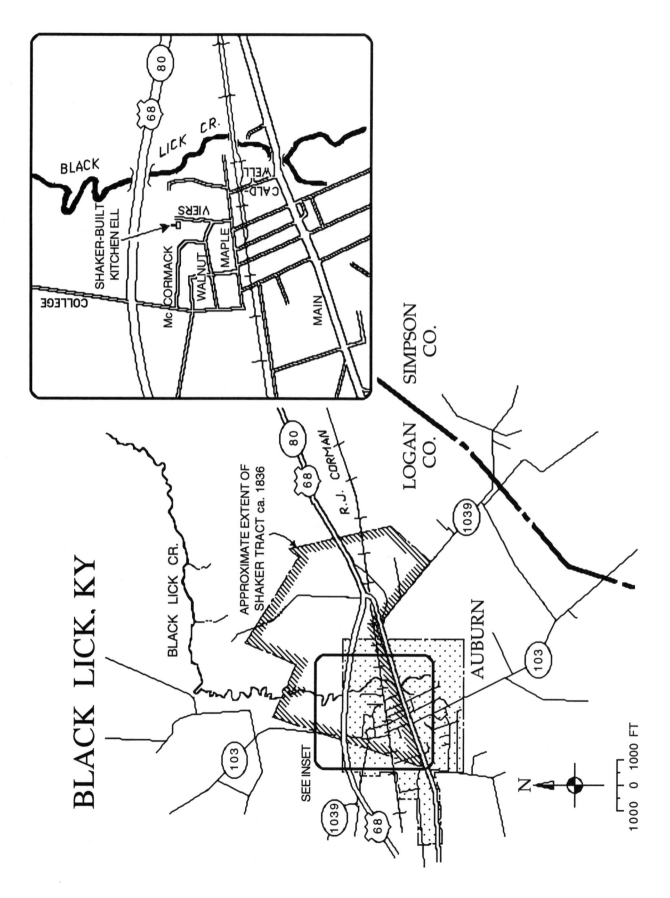

BLACK LICK, KY

BLACK LICK CR.

APPROXIMATE EXTENT OF SHAKER TRACT ca. 1836

SEE INSET

R.J. CORMAN

AUBURN

SIMPSON CO.

LOGAN CO.

1039

103

1039

68

80

68

N

1000 0 1000 FT

Inset:

BLACK

LICK CR.

80

68

CALD-WELL

VIERS

SHAKER-BUILT KITCHEN ELL

McCORMACK

WALNUT

MAPLE

MAIN

COLLEGE

Rankin and Eli McLean sold 219 acres of their property west of Black Lick Creek to a prosperous local farmer, John Viers. Then in 1859 the Louisville and Nashville Railroad purchased a right of way on the Shaker land east of Black Lick Creek.

Viers and two other individuals acquired 708 acres south of the Bowling Green-Russellville Road known as Federal Grove in 1860. It was on portions of this land and Viers' earlier purchase from the Shakers that the plan for Auburn was drawn. Auburn was incorporated in 1865.[14] Within a few years, a grist mill and granary, tannery, warehouse, churches, a school, stores, and residences sprang up.

Sometime between 1838 and 1860, Viers attached a two-story, I-house[15]—possibly on a Shaker foundation—to the kitchen ell of an old Shaker dwelling. Curry and Deedy Hall purchased this home in the 1930s. Living in the house with its Shaker ell coupled with her own memories of the South Union Shakers sparked Mrs. Hall's interest in collecting furniture and artifacts from the South Union community.

During the 1960s she turned an old church, ca. 1871, on their property into the "Shaker Museum Inc." where the Shaker pieces could be enjoyed by the public. Her outstanding collection was moved from Auburn in 1971 to the 1824 Centre House at South Union which had recently been acquired by Shakertown Revisited, Inc. It forms the backbone of the western Shaker furnishings on display there. The old church which housed Mrs. Hall's museum stands on the southwest corner of Viers and Walnut Streets.

Dale Covington

"the very remotest corner of the gospel vineyard."

Drakes Creek
Warren County, Kentucky

South Union had successfully established two sawmills, one fulling mill, and one gristmill at its Logan County site and wished to expand this type of activity into other areas. In January 1817 John Rankin, Benjamin Seth Youngs, and Joseph Allen visited a site in nearby Warren County, 16 miles from their home base. From a bluff overlooking Drakes Creek, they viewed a meandering waterway, fertile bottom lands, and fine timberlands and sensed a prosperous new enterprise. That same month they purchased the mill site and 300 surrounding acres.[16]

Additional land was acquired over the next few years. By 1820 their ownership in Warren County amounted to 1,274 acres, costing the community $8,780. The new area was known as Mill Point.

The Shakers had trouble getting a permit to build a mill on the site. In March 1817 a jury appointed by the court examined the site and condemned the "mill seat." The trustees took the matter to a higher court. With a petition containing 1,200 signatures of neighbors, Samuel Whyte went to the state capital in January 1818. He came back to South Union with the news that the decision favored the society. Construction began at the site.[17]

A group moved from South Union to build and operate the mill. It was recorded: "Apr. 14—1818—Ho! For Drakes Creek—a proper big move—Three sisters go to cook. Two wagon loads of furniture & provision— Also Saml. Shannon & Black Matt. John Rankin goes to begin the orchard."[18] They kept in contact with the rest of the community by returning each Saturday to attend meetings on the Sabbath. Even Rankin walked the 16 miles home from Mill Point in his 71st year.

South Union's determination to make a financial success of their Drakes Creek mill was not to be. Workers noticed that in the dry weather the water in the stream would disappear in great sink holes so that it was not available for operating the mill. Filling the sink holes was expensive and fairly useless. The mill could be operated only seasonally. The Shakers had to keep the stream open for navigation. A canal was considered, but the expense would have required neighbors to help subsidize it. By 1829 the South Union Shakers sold the property for $8,000. They had put $30,000 into it. It was their first financial disaster.

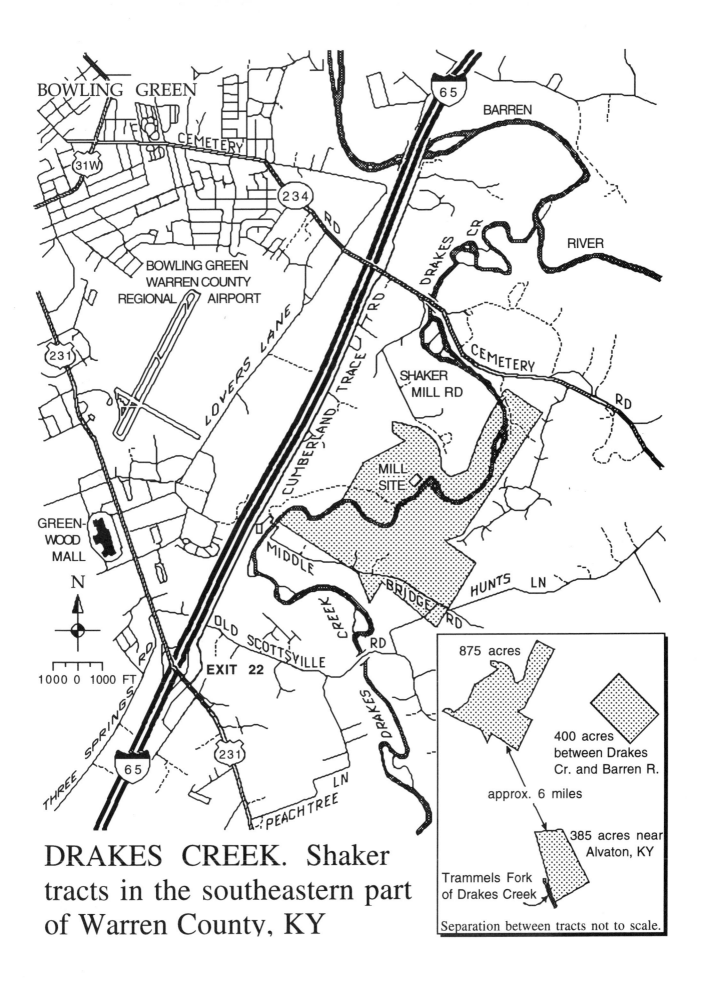

DRAKES CREEK. Shaker tracts in the southeastern part of Warren County, KY

875 acres

400 acres between Drakes Cr. and Barren R.

approx. 6 miles

385 acres near Alvaton, KY

Trammels Fork of Drakes Creek

Separation between tracts not to scale.

59

Years later as he was copying Youngs' diary into *Record A*, Elder Hervey Eades summarized the Drakes Creek enterprise:

> *The purchasing...was a magnificent blunder–It has cost immense treasure, to build it up–But the fact early discovered, that the water escaping under the Bluff for 1/4 mile should have deterred further prosecution of the Work–In loss of souls–by sickness & estrangement & loss on Money all together is not easily computed.*[19]

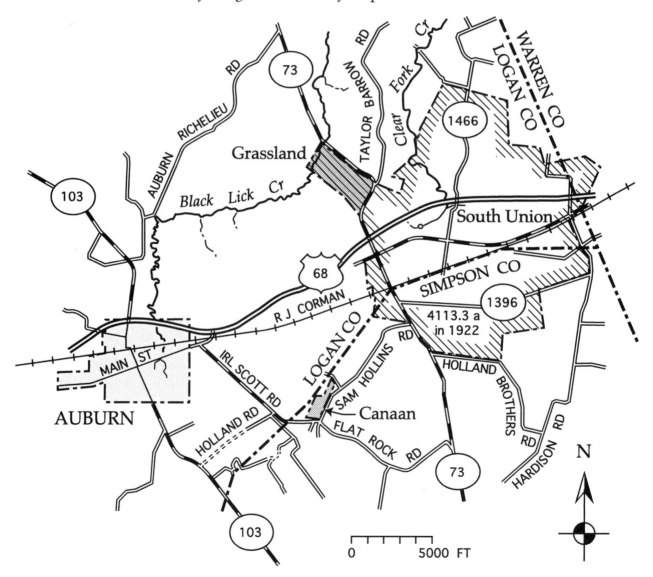

SOUTH UNION: CANAAN AND GRASSLAND

The land was particularly suited for peach and cherry orchards.

Canaan and Grassland
Simpson and Logan Counties, Kentucky

Canaan and Grassland were outfarms acquired by South Union in the 1850s. Canaan began as one of two 18-acre tracts mutually exchanged between the South Union Shakers and David Lowe in February 1857. Within days the brethren were planting peach trees on their latest acquisition. The land was particularly suited for peach and cherry orchards.[20]

As the orchards matured, the Shakers found it advisable to stay at Canaan to care for the ripening fruit and guard it from "Neighbor depredations." Vacating the farm during the winter also proved costly. At peach worming time in 1864, the Shakers discovered their house at Canaan was broken open, ransacked, and robbed of everything of value which had been left when the fruit harvest was over.[21]

The family at Canaan under the leadership of elderly George Rankin in the 1860s was not numerically large. By November 1866 just four people lived there.[22]

The undulating terrain and orchards at Canaan made this a picturesque place for rides with visiting Shaker ministries. In 1876 the farm, by now encompassing 40 acres, was surveyed for sale at a proposed selling price of $30 an acre.[23] The transaction was finalized 10 years later.

The Trustees purchased the 210-acre tract they called Grassland at auction for $14.80 an acre late in 1850. In addition to providing pasture for horses and cattle, the farm was also used to raise wheat. During the war years there were infrequent encounters between blacks living on the farm and Federal and Confederate troops passing through on the Morgantown and Franklin Road.[24] Grassland was included in the 4,113.3 acres of land in Logan, Simpson, and Warren Counties that the Shakers sold when South Union closed in 1922.

Dale Covington and Mike Sisk

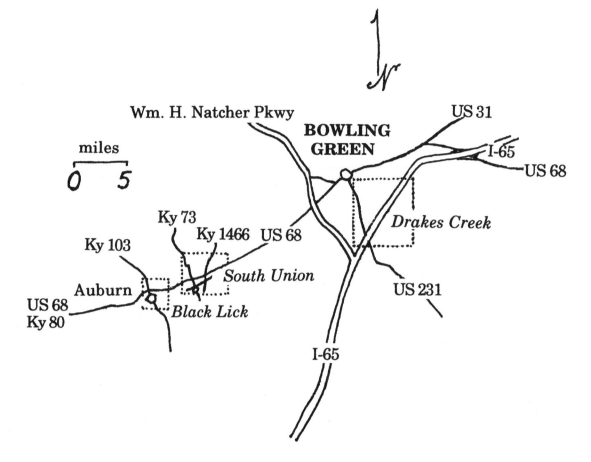

Planning Your Visit to South Union

There are special activities planned throughout the year which make South Union a rewarding destination. A seminar with outstanding speakers is held annually in April. An herbal fair, candlelight dinners, a Shaker breakfast as well as a Summer Shaker Festival will enrich your visits. For a calendar of events, call the museum at (502) 542-4167 or write to the Shaker Museum, South Union, KY 42283. Those on-line can visit South Union's Web page at http://www.logantele.com/~shakmus/ or use shakmus@logantele.com for e-mail inquiries.

The museum's season begins March 1 with weekday hours 9 A.M. to 5 P.M. Sunday hours are 1 P.M. to 5 P.M. The museum is closed Thanksgiving weekend and ends its season on December 15. Off-season visits may be arranged by appointment. Admission fees: Adults $4, Children $1, members free. There are special rates for groups and reservations are required.

To arrange an overnight stay at the Shaker Tavern on Route 73, one and a half miles from the museum, call for information: (502) 542-6801.

[1] *South Union Record A*, October 15 to November 19, 1807, 81.

[2] Benjamin Seth Youngs, letter to Ministry, New Lebanon, New York, May 2, 1813, WRHS IV:A-60.

[3] A group located on land at a distance from the main community property.

[4] *Record A*, January 1, 1814, 130.

[5] *South Union Record C*, January 1, 1867, 99.

[6] Julia Neal, *The Kentucky Shakers* (Lexington: University Press of Kentucky, 1977), 61-73.

[7] Julia Neal, editor, *The Journal of Eldress Nancy* (Nashville: Parthenon Press, 1963), 77-79, 110-11.

[8] *Record C*, January 1, 1867 and February 13, 1874, 99 and 380.

[9] *US Census Schedules*, Logan County, Kentucky.

[10] Stephen J. Stein, *The Shaker Experience in America* (New Haven, Connecticut: Yale University Press, 1992), 255-56.

[11] *Record A*, 139.

[12] Ibid., 144.

[13] *South Union Record B*, August 29-September 2, 1837, 35-36.

[14] Edward Coffman, *The Story of Logan County* (Nashville: The Parthenon Press, 1962), 266-72; Auburn Historic District, Logan County, Kentucky, application for the National Register of Historic Places, December 22, 1993, on file at Kentucky Heritage Council, Frankfort, Kentucky; *Atlas of Logan County* (Dayton: Wright & Son, 1877).

[15] An I-house is one room deep, two full stories, with the entrance in the long side.

[16] Donna Parker, "'Ho! for Drakes Creek:' Something Ventured, Nothing Gained," *Journal of the Communal Studies Association* 14 (1994): 113.

[17] Julia Neal, *By Their Fruits: Shakerism at South Union* (1947; reprint, Philadelphia: Porcupine Press, 1975), 85-86.

[18] *Record A*, 260.

[19] Ibid., May 2, 1829, 442.

[20] *Record B*, February 26, 1857, 235.

[21] Neal, *Journal of Eldress Nancy*, 195

[22] *Record C*, November 12, 1866, 193.

[23] Ibid., November 30, 1876, 454.

[24] Neal, *Journal of Eldress Nancy*, 91, 92, 111.

Chapter 12

Red Banks

Henderson County, Kentucky

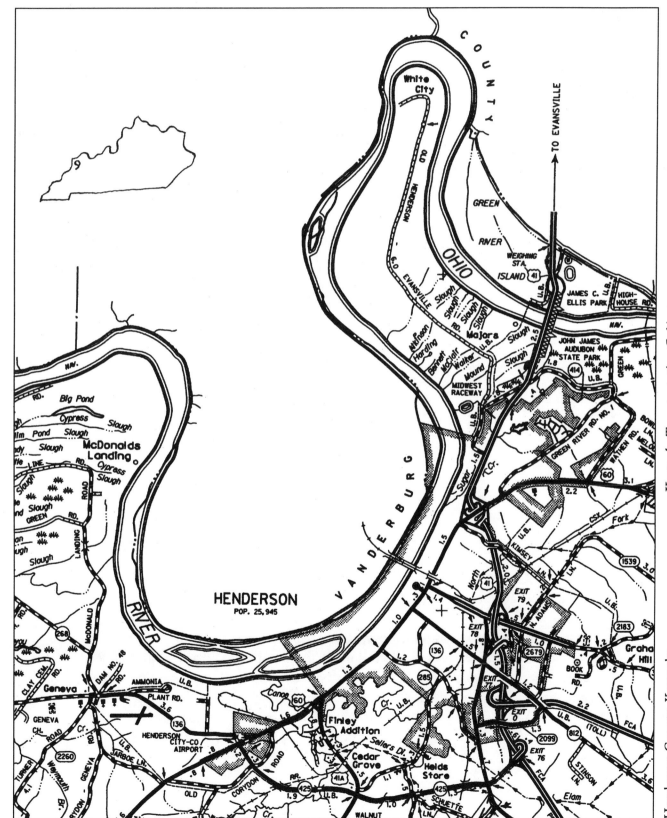

Kentucky Transportation Cabinet

Henderson County, Kentucky

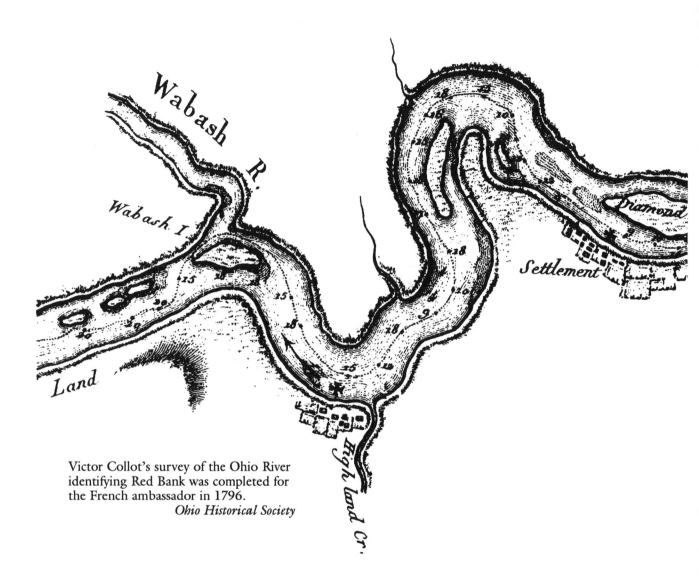

Victor Collot's survey of the Ohio River identifying Red Bank was completed for the French ambassador in 1796.
Ohio Historical Society

A letter dated January 30, 1801, about the strength of the revival is quoted by Richard McNemar in his book, *The Kentucky Revival*: "The work is still increasing in Cumberland: It has overspread the whole country. It is in Nashville, Barren, Muddy, Gasper, Redbanks, Knoxville, &c."

In addition to being a site for the fervor of the Kentucky Revival, Red Banks was a popular crossing point along the Ohio River when trips were made between South Union in Kentucky and Busro in Indiana.

A gathering of about 30 Shaker converts in Red Bank grew from the efforts of John McComb. His half-bother, Jesse McComb, had worked with

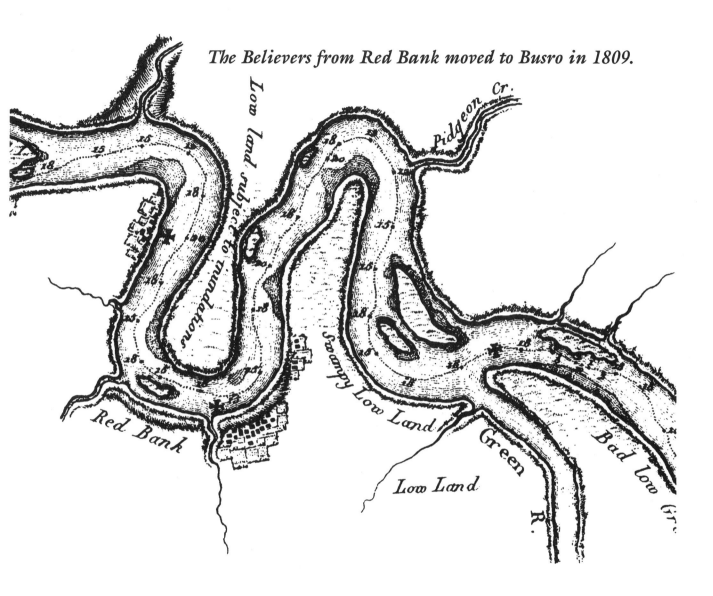

The Believers from Red Bank moved to Busro in 1809.

John Rankin in the establishment of South Union. Benjamin Seth Youngs wrote in his journal in the fall of 1807, "[At Gasper] By appointment we went to Jno. Shannons & preached. 1st Confession—John McComb of Red Bank."[1] The Believers from Red Bank moved to Busro in 1809.

Red Bank or Red Banks is now part of the city of Henderson, where "red banks" still survives as a place name. There's Red Bank Tower and Red Banks Old Folks Home in downtown Henderson.

---

[1] *South Union Record A*, October 27, 1807, 83.

Chapter 13

Busro or West Union
Knox and Sullivan Counties, Indiana

As the pioneers of Ohio and Kentucky continued to migrate west, so did new Shaker converts. In 1808 some of these converts were living along the Wabash River near Vincennes, Indiana, in sufficient numbers for Union Village, Ohio, to send five Shakers, including Issachar Bates, to minister to them and to convert others.

A new community was ready to gather in Knox County on the Wabash River by 1809. When David Darrow of Union Village asked Issachar Bates about the feasibility of Busro (also known as West Union after 1816), Bates said he didn't know why anyone would want to live in the Wabash

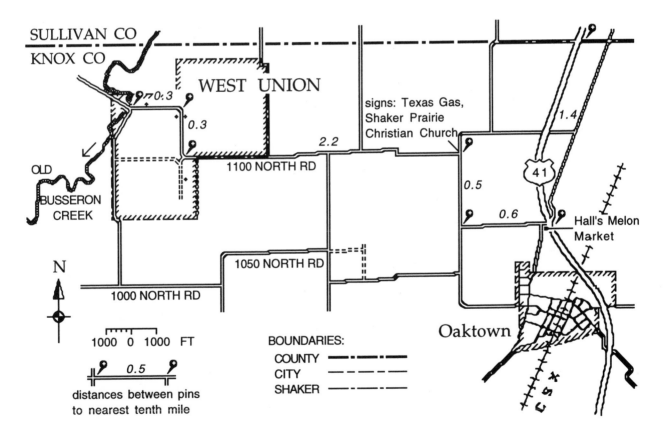

WEST UNION AND OAKTOWN, IN

Valley as it was full of heathens and malcontents, as well as malaria. He remarked, "It will take the wisest man on earth to lead that society." Darrow's answer was to send Bates to be an elder at West Union.[1] That year, 30 Believers from Red Banks, Kentucky, also took up residence there.

The Shakers at West Union were beginning to flourish by 1811. They had gathered into three families over a seven-mile area containing 1,300 acres. They also had additional acreage in Sullivan County to the north. Most of this land was scattered between Busseron Creek and what are now Routes 41 and 150 south of Carlisle.[2]

In the early years malaria caused much suffering at Busro. In a letter from there, a sister from Union Village wrote that she had come with a hundred other brethren and sisters; within three months, there were only 80 of them; by the end of six months, only 45 of the group were still alive. That year the ministry at Union Village decided to send Believers from the struggling Ohio communities of Eagle Creek and Straight Creek to West Union. They arrived just in time for the awesome New Madrid earthquake which occurred in a series of shocks from December 1811 to mid-February 1812. By the fall of 1812 there were serious Indian troubles as well.

William Henry Harrison, governor of Indiana, purchased the middle third of Indiana from the Miami Indians. Tecumseh and his brother, the Prophet, and other Indian tribes maintained that it was not the Miamis' land to sell. Governor Harrison brought the militia through West Union en route to a battle with the Indians camped on the Tippecanoe River. The militia disliked the Shakers because they were pacifists who refused to participate in military activities. The militia defeated the Indians, but by that time the country was at war with England. It was feared that Indiana would become a major battlefield, so the Union Village ministry recalled the West Union Shakers.

With much difficulty some of the Busro members floated, sailed, and poled a keelboat down the Wabash and up the Ohio River to take their possessions to Union Village. Most of the 300 to 400 brethren and sisters from Busro, however, traveled by land with 14 wagons, 100 head of cattle, and 250 head of sheep. Struggling with continual rains and muddy roads, the Shakers went on foot first to South Union and then to Pleasant Hill in their long journey to Union Village. Nearly two months passed before both groups reached Union Village.

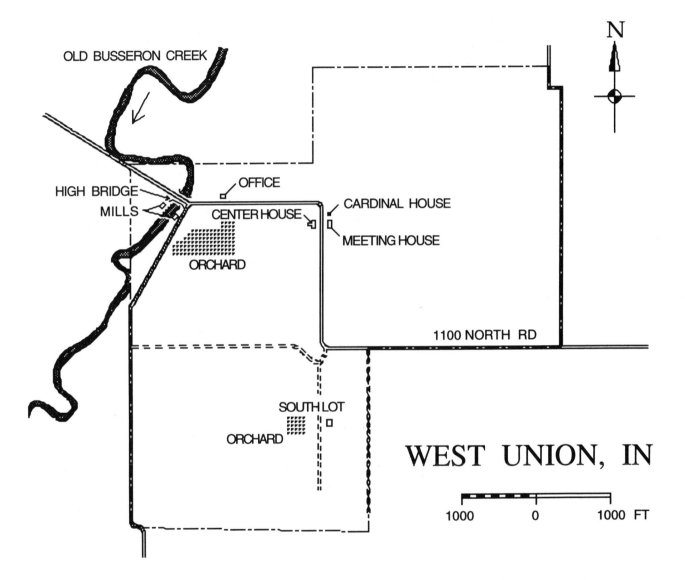

OLD BUSSERON CREEK

HIGH BRIDGE
MILLS

OFFICE

CENTER HOUSE

CARDINAL HOUSE

MEETING HOUSE

ORCHARD

1100 NORTH RD

SOUTH LOT

ORCHARD

WEST UNION, IN

1000   0   1000 FT

Not until the spring of 1814 was it deemed safe for the brethren and sisters to return to Busro. The trip back home was an easier move, but they found that the militia had destroyed much of the village. As they rebuilt, they consolidated near Busseron Creek.

Elder Issachar Bates wrote to Brother Seth Y. Wells (in late spring of 1815):

> *The Believers are accommodated in four dwelling houses, the Center House, the North, West, and South Houses, not more than 50 rods*

It is in truth the easiest and best place to get a living that I ever saw...

from the Center House. The Society is in a comfortable state of health, except common infirmities and all are doing tolerably well...We will not relate what we have suffered through the fall and winter before we got these buildings prepared. Nay we will forget it for we have food and rainment and no apprehensions of want, but to the contrary a good prospect of crops for this is a goodly land.

I can this moment lift my eyes at this window toward the east and survey four or five miles of beautiful green grassy plains sprinkled with cattle and sheep in hundreds and most that are in sight belong to Believers. The most beautiful sight nature ever exhibited. I can look out the west window and see more than a hundred acres equally green with wheat, oats and barley and a beautiful young orchard of about eight hundred young apple trees, the greater part of which are now shedding their blossoms, and about six hundred peach trees with more fruit on most of them than they can bear... If I go south, I can walk nearly a mile on ground that is now in preparation for planting corn. If I go north, there is a large field—but I will stop...

It is in truth the easiest and best place to get a living that I ever saw....[3]

Absolem H. Blackburn lived at West Union from June 1823 to the end of January 1824. He published in his apostate account of 1824 this view of the community:

The population of this society is moderate, not exceeding two hundred ....Their new meeting house, and center house, are in the same order of those as Union Village. They have a grist mill, saw mill, carding machine, fulling-mill, flax machine, cotton-gin all are by water. They have also a distillery & shops of various kinds.[4]

For several years the Indiana legislature attempted to find a way to compel the Shakers either to participate in the militia or to pay the fines. In 1824 they enacted a statute that held a community responsible for the fines of its members who refused militia duty. The Shakers were prosperous in land and goods, but had little hard cash. So the Shakers once more sadly packed their goods and left the village permanently in 1827, going to Pleasant Hill, South Union, Union Village, and White Water.

The property in Knox County was sold in 1835 to the Springer family.[5] At the time some of the buildings remained. In 1870 the dwelling house was dismantled and the materials were used to build a large Italianate mansion. In 1890 the meetinghouse was demolished. By the 1980s, the Springers were gone and the mansion was collapsing. It was bulldozed in 1992.

The only visible Shaker imprint on the landscape is a unique pecan-hickory tree, said to have been planted by the Shakers.

Dorothy Jones

[1] Issachar Bates, *Autobiography*, 1832, 59.

[2] Letter from John Martin Smith to Martha Boice, February 5, 1996.

[3] John Martin Smith, "The Shaker Community at West Union located at Busro, Indiana" (talk presented to the Western Shaker Study Group, Lebanon, Ohio, October 5, 1990).

[4] Absolem H. Blackburn, *A Brief Account of the People Usually Denominated Shakers* (1824; reprint, with an introduction by Elizabeth A. DeWolfe, Ashfield, Massachusetts: Huntstown Press, 1996), 21.

[5] The land in Sullivan County was sold by about 1837, according to the letter from John Martin Smith, February 5, 1996.

Ambrau, Illinois and Oaktown, Indiana

...the river raised very high and the water broke round the abutment at the grist mill and the river soon took its course there and left the grist mill standing near the middle of the river...

Chapter 14

Ambrau
Lawrence County, Illinois

The westernmost Shaker settlement was a mill site and community related to West Union. Ambrau was located 18 miles west of Busro in Lawrence County, Illinois, on the Embarras River. (*Embarras* is a French word meaning "clogged" and is pronounced "ambrau.") The Shakers owned five quarter sections of land or 800 acres at Ambrau. The mill site was active from about 1811 to 1820.

To get to the Ambrau site, go south from Oaktown on Route 41 to Route 50 in Vincennes. Go west on Route 50, crossing the Wabash River, to Lawrenceville. In Lawrenceville, take Route 1 north to Birds. Go west on Route 10 from Birds to a bridge crossing the Embarras River. The mill site, about 1,000 feet to the north of the bridge, is on the east side of the river. In low water it is possible to see some remnants of the beams from the mill. There is a good view from a nearby bluff. The Shaker community of Ambrau was located a distance north of the mill site and included at least two major dwelling houses.[1]

As you cast your eyes northward from the bridge, read this account describing the work that the brethren did at Ambrau:

> *July 17th. [1820] Some time previous the water had broke under the dam at Ambau which now had to be repaired—for which purpose Samuel McClelland and James Mead with some other brethren went out to Ambrau and stayed, from six weeks to two months, during which time they went through a pritty heavy job of repareing at the Mills—part of which was an addition to the forebay, and a new water wheel for the grist mill—faceing and dressing the stones—new cogs in the spur wheel—new bolting reel and chest—and a number of other fixings—Also made a new breast for the sawmill and sank the wheel 22 inches—made a new pitmon—and many of the repairs—after which the mills done good business for a short time—till the river raised very high and the water broke round the abutment at the grist mill and the river soon took its course there and left the grist mill standing near the middle of the river—after which it was rented to Alva Beacher—and again to Colonal Heath of Ohio—And finally the Society lost—or nearly the whole possession—However there was but very little ever paid for it—after 5 or six years trouble and disappointment.[2]*

---

[1] Smith, "The Shaker Community at West Union located at Busro, Indiana."

[2] Samuel Swan McClelland, "Memorandum of Remarkable Events," in J.P. MacLean, *Shakers of Ohio*, 317-318.

Chapter 15

Darby Plains
Union and Champaign Counties, Ohio

In June 1820 reports reached the Union Village Shakers of a religious fervor on the Darby Plains in Union County, Ohio, about 70 miles to the north and east. Elder David Darrow, alert to the possibilities of attracting new members, dispatched Richard McNemar and Calvin Morrell to see what was happening at Darby Plains. Douglas Farnum,[1] their leader, greeted the Shakers enthusiastically, telling them about the group's revival work in central Ohio.

The visit was returned later in the summer when Douglas Farnum, Samuel Rice Sr., and Elijah Bacon traveled to Union Village. Farnum addressed the group on Sunday morning and impressed those who heard him. Rice also made a good impression on the Union Village Shakers. They wrote of him, "His unfeigned simplicity and honesty created in all who conversed with him universal esteem and goodwill. He drank deep of the living waters, and appeared to be perfectly satisfied with our testimony."[2]

These Farnhamites, as they were called, were colorfully portrayed in Union County histories. A Burnham family member recalled occasionally attending their meetings at Rice City, Ohio:[3] "They generally had preaching on Sunday, unless Farnham was away. They held night and sometimes day meetings through the week; some of them were quiet, social prayer meetings, some for confessing their sins, and some for hugging and kissing each other. . . .[They met] at the log schoolhouse, where the brick meeting house now stands, on the pike from Milford to Irwin. . ."[4]

Historical chronicler Henry Howe asked noted journalist, William Henry Smith, to recall the early days in Union County. Smith wrote,

> *Our county was not free from eccentric people, but their eccentricity took on the character of religious fanaticism. These were the Farnhamites (also called "The Creepers"), followers of Douglas Farnham. . . . I could tell you many anecdotes of the Farnhamites, if we had the leisure and it were profitable. One will do. . . .The leaders taught the birth to sin, and salvation only through public confession and walking humbly and contritely before the world. The fanaticism consisted in the absurd acts which were inspired and performed. Sackcloth and ashes and creeping in the dirt were not the most objectionable. An estimable young lady was converted, and told that it was necessary to display the corrupt nature of her heart. She conceived this novel plan. One night she rode several miles to the farm of a well-known citizen, visited his corn-crib, filled a bag with corn,*

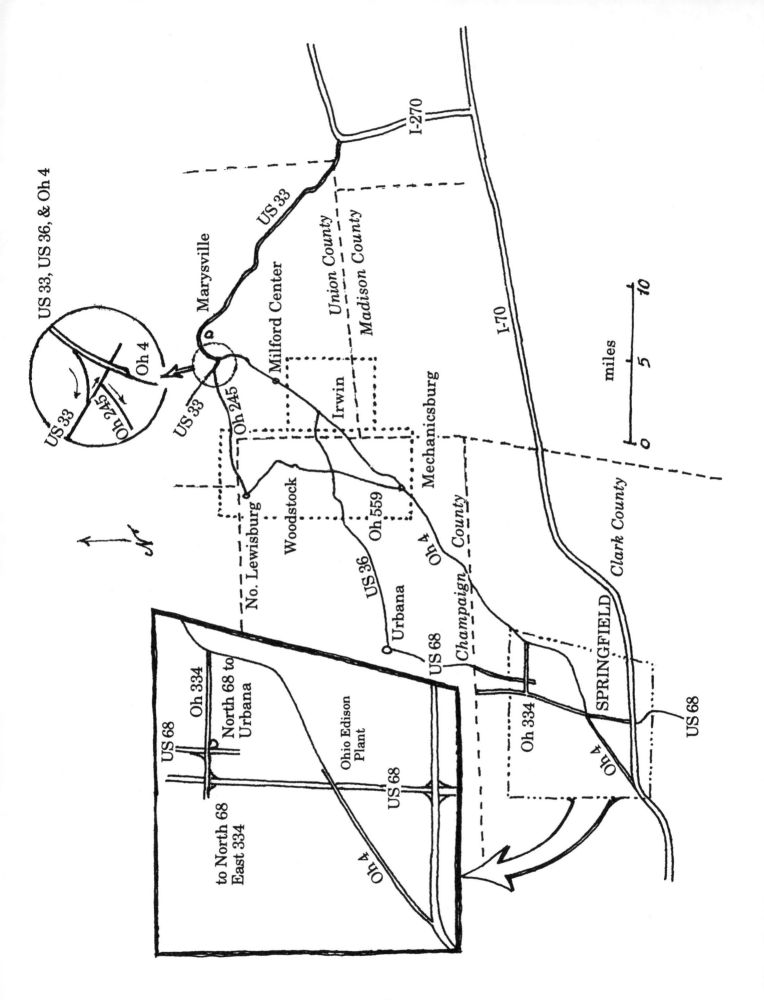

which she carried home. The next day, in the light of the sun, this bag of corn was placed upon the back of a horse, and upon that the young lady rode to the farmer's, to whom she confessed the theft in contrite words and with many tears. This fanaticism soon disappeared and left no evil effects, as it touched only a handful in the community.[5]

These Darby Plains Farnhamites had their roots in Rhode Island near the Connecticut line. An intertwined group of families with surnames including Bates, Cranston, Burlingame, and Rice in Rice City, Rhode Island, became followers of the charismatic leader, Douglas Farnum. Their church affiliation bound these families in a movement which took them from Rhode Island to central Ohio.

The story of their oddessy began in 1796 when William Rice and his bother, Samuel, purchased land to build an inn on the Plainfield Turnpike, a main route between Providence, Rhode Island, and Norwich, Connecticut. Samuel, the tavern keeper and a gambler and drunkard, was the one who invited Elder Farnum to come to Rice City from Vermont in 1812. It was quite a shock to the community when Rice and several others listening to the powerful message by the charismatic Farnum were baptized and formed a church in January 1813. The group became known as "Farnhamites." Performing acts of contrition such as donning sack cloth and ashes before baptism were an integral part of their religious experience.[6]

Farnum left Rice City to go on missionary trips into Connecticut, Vermont, New York, and other areas of Rhode Island. He returned in 1815 to find his flock in "perilous circumstances," there being many trials and difficulties among them. In reorganizing his church, Farnum decided to send Samuel Rice, the clerk of his church association, to the Darby Plains in central Ohio in the spring of 1815. In June 1817 Elder Farnum and Nathan Burlingame also journeyed to Ohio with a number of church members. They joined forces with Samuel Rice and soon baptized about 100 persons in the Darby Plains area. In August of that year, Farnum purchased about 125 acres of land in Union Township, Union County near Route 4 and Conner Road.

In the fall of 1817 Farnum, Burlingame, and Archibald Bates returned to Connecticut to organize a church in Hampton. Members of this church brought charges against Farnum the following spring. There were rumors that he had three wives and was an impostor, not an ordained minister. He had advanced warning that a hearing was to take place and

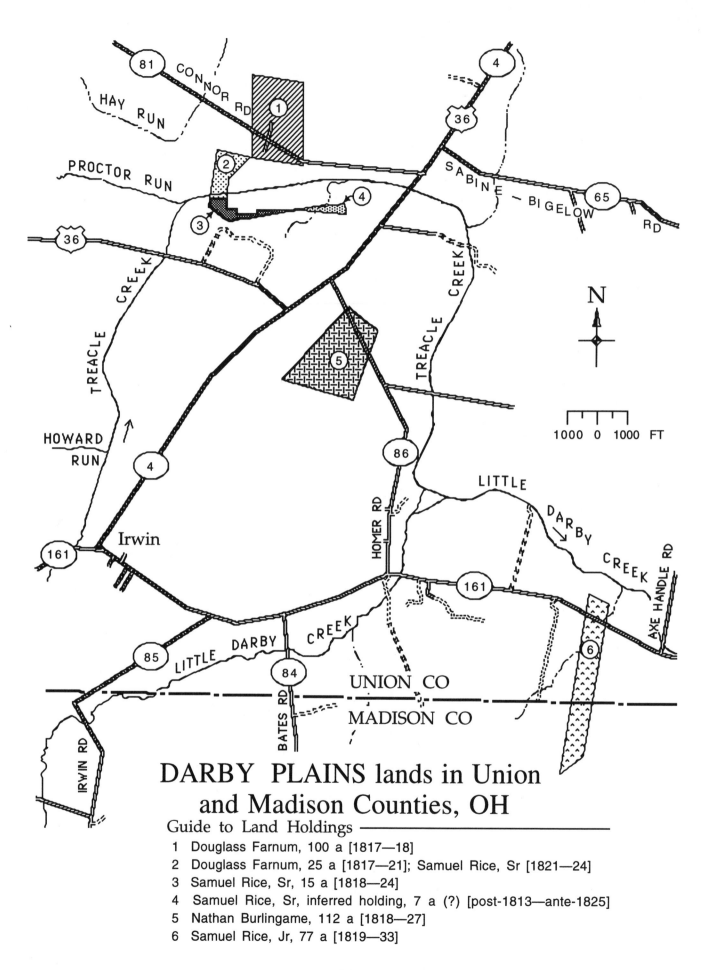

DARBY PLAINS lands in Union and Madison Counties, OH

Guide to Land Holdings ─────────

1 Douglass Farnum, 100 a [1817—18]
2 Douglass Farnum, 25 a [1817—21]; Samuel Rice, Sr [1821—24]
3 Samuel Rice, Sr, 15 a [1818—24]
4 Samuel Rice, Sr, inferred holding, 7 a (?) [post-1813—ante-1825]
5 Nathan Burlingame, 112 a [1818—27]
6 Samuel Rice, Jr, 77 a [1819—33]

In Union County the Farnhamites owned land in three Virginia Military Surveys...

brought letters attesting to his ordination and character. The charges were not sustained. That same spring (1818) during his stay in the East, Farnum sold 100 acres of Ohio land in Union County to Asa Bates of Coventry, Rhode Island. Then on September 1, 1818, he sold his home at Rice City. Nathan Burlingame, Archibald L. Bates, and other active members of his church accompanied Farnum and his family as they left for Ohio a final time.

In Union County the Farnhamites owned land in three Virginia Military Surveys:[7] Nathan Burlingame owned 112 acres in Survey 7789; Samuel Rice Jr. owned 77 acres in Survey 7474; and both Samuel Rice Sr. and Douglas Farnum owned small acreages in Survey 5708, near Route 4 (the road from Milford to Irwin) and Conner Road.[8]

After the visits in 1820 with Union Village Shakers, Farnum withdrew from the group in Union County and purchased 80 acres of land in what would become Marion County, north of Columbus. He completed the payment for this land just a few weeks before he died on the Plains of Sandusky (between Marion and Bucyrus, Ohio) in January 1822.[9] It was reported that he was found in a "quagmire," and it was not known if he fell from his horse or some foul play was involved. He was an itinerant to the end.[10]

Land purchases in neighboring Rush Township, Champaign County, took place shortly after this exchange of visits.[11] Samuel Rice Sr. and his friend, John Cranston, purchased two Virginia Military Surveys totaling 1,100 acres in September 1820. The next month they deeded land to each other to create two farms, Rice owning 500 acres and Cranston, 600. Pleasant Run crossed Rice's plantation. With this move to Champaign County, Samuel Rice and Burlingame became the leaders of the religious group.

Visits continued between the Farnhamites and the Shakers. Union Village Shakers Calvin Morrell, a physician, and Samuel Sering traveled to the Plains early in October 1822. It was just a few weeks later that a letter from Rice came to Union Village that many on the Plains were sick with a fever. A terrifying epidemic had struck and "many who a few weeks before were rugged and cheerful, were now reduced to skeletons. . ." Morrell and Sering returned for three weeks to assist.[12]

Burlingame made his first visit to Union Village in November 1822. He cast his lot with the Shakers. As an influential minister, he persuaded many to follow his lead.

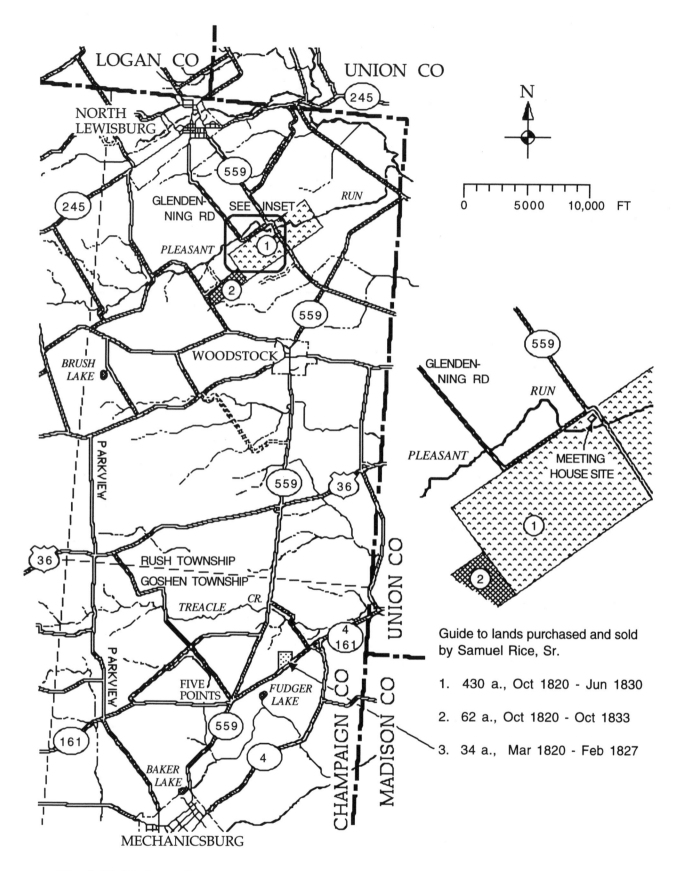

Guide to lands purchased and sold
by Samuel Rice, Sr.

1.   430 a., Oct 1820 - Jun 1830

2.   62 a., Oct 1820 - Oct 1833

3.   34 a., Mar 1820 - Feb 1827

DARBY PLAINS. Champaign Co., OH

...the Shaker leadership at Union Village realized that the Darby settlement required "profound attention."

By the spring of 1823, the decision was made by the Union Village Shakers to form a community at Darby Plains on the plantation of Samuel Rice. At the same time they instructed Burlingame to give up his land in Survey 7789 to Martin Simmons and Gideon Brownell, who had very limited resources. In trips to Darby Plains, Union Village Shakers found the people in high spirits, determined to work in union and obedience. There was great optimism about establishing a community. By August 1823 Morrell and Samuel Sering were assisting the Darby Plains group in building a meetinghouse for its 40 members.[13]

That fall, however, the Shaker leadership at Union Village realized that the Darby settlement required "profound attention." Again a dreadful malaria epidemic erupted on the Plains.[14] The Shaker leadership weighed the consequences of repeated times of illness as well as the uncertainty of their land titles in a military district, against the opportunities to establish a fledgling society at a more desirable locality at White Water, Ohio. In December 1823, the Shakers dispatched Morrell and Stephen Williams to the Plains to share with them "the gift" of moving to the developing White Water community. In January, Morrell visited again, securing money to invest at White Water. Samuel Rice Sr. provided most of the funds.[15]

After the decision to relocate at the White Water Shaker community, Burlingame along with Morrell traveled to central Ohio to find Douglas Farnum's widow, Susan, and daughter, Louisa. With much persuasion, they convinced them to move to White Water.

The next month Burlingame packed his possessions into a two-horse wagon and was on his way to White Water. Other Darby Plains members began arriving at White Water. Transfers continued during the summer and "near a year had elapsed before all got down." From 1824 to 1833 various tracts in Union and Champaign Counties were sold by the Rices and Burlingame. Today Samuel Rice's 500-acre plantation is still rich Ohio farmland traversed by Pleasant Run, but evidence of the meeting house in Champaign County has been obliterated.

[1] Also spelled Farnham and Farnam

[2] J.P. MacLean, *Shakers of Ohio*, 231. MacLean depended almost entirely on a now missing manuscript by Elder Charles Sturr of the White Water Shaker community to create the story of the Darby Plains Shakers. Sturr had rescued parts of the church family record from the Center Family dwelling coal bin and copied the records into a separate book. He also copied into the book other manuscripts and diaries of the early Darby Plains Shakers. Unfortunately Sturr's compilation has vanished and the MacLean account is the primary source of information about this central Ohio Shaker community.

[3] Rice City, Ohio, was a squatters' town southwest of Milford Center between Conner Road and Route 36, west of Route 4. Union County historian, Rachel Robinson. Letter to the author February 6, 1995.

[4] W.H. Beers, *History of Union County*, Ohio (Chicago: 1883), V, 181.

[5] Henry Howe, *Historical Collections of Ohio* (Cincinnati:1888), II, 716.

[6] Michael Dallas Morse, "Farnamites" (A family research project, n.d.)

[7] The Virginia Military District consisted of land between the Little Miami and Scioto Rivers set aside to satisfy military bounty warrants for the State of Virginia. Claims could be made for services in the Revolutionary War as well as the French and Indian Wars. Described by "metes and bounds" (indiscriminate), the surveys of the more than 4,000,000 acres created a patchwork of surveys. Because of the vast number of surveys and the difficulty in finding the physical objects they relied upon, there are probably more court cases about boundaries in this area than any other in Ohio.

[8] See Appendix III for the description of a computer program developed in this study to unravel the complexities encountered in deed research. Included is a detailed application of the analytical approach in identifying lands of the Darby Plains Farnhamites in Virginia Military Survey 5708.

[9] National Archives and Records Administration, Washington, DC. Cash entry for Patent No. 906, Delaware [Ohio] Land Office, (April 4, 1822); *Will Book 1*, Delaware County, OH (January 23, 1822), 20-22.

[10] Agnes A. Arnold, "From Rice City, R. I. to Ohio" (Paper given at the meeting of the Western Rhode Island Civic Historical Society in Rice City, Rhode Island, April 28, 1953)

[11] Prior to this purchase, Samuel Rice acquired 34 acres in Goshen Township, Champaign County, Ohio, on March 14, 1820. See Champaign County map.

[12] MacLean, 231.

[13] Location of the meetinghouse identified by Ed Ridder, *Champaign County Landmark Atlas* (Urbana, Ohio: Main Graphics, 1979), 55; telephone conversation with author, December 7, 1996.

[14] Carolyn V. Platt, "Prairie Remnants of the Darby Plains," *Timeline 1*, no. 1 (1984): 46.

[15] MacLean, 234.

Chapter 16

White Water

Butler and Hamilton Counties, Ohio

The origins of White Water trace back to a small group of settlers in southern Butler County, Ohio, who gathered together as Shakers in 1822, possibly earlier. In 1823, the members of three prominent Butler County families joined, and this community (which had no formal name) moved to a larger farm. Undoubtedly at the urging of an early convert, Miriam Agnew, the Union Village ministry increased its spiritual and material support for White Water, culminating in the first purchase of land for White Water by Union Village trustees in 1824.

The newly gathered Believers were joined in 1824 by the Darby Plains Shakers, whose former New Light and Farnhamite preacher, Nathan Burlingame, was the first to arrive at White Water from that abandoned central Ohio community.

The first years were difficult because their few acres were forested and poor for farming. Noting the deprivations of the group, Calvin Morrell wrote later at Union Village, "It was Lent with them nearly all year round."[1] In 1825, however, the Shakers were able to purchase 215 acres of good land for a mill seat on the Dry Fork of the White Water River, and the new community moved again to the site of the White Water North Family. Union Village brethren arrived in 1826 to help establish the family. The brick Meeting House was completed in 1827, the same year that the Shakers' saw mill on

Oxford Road White Water

85

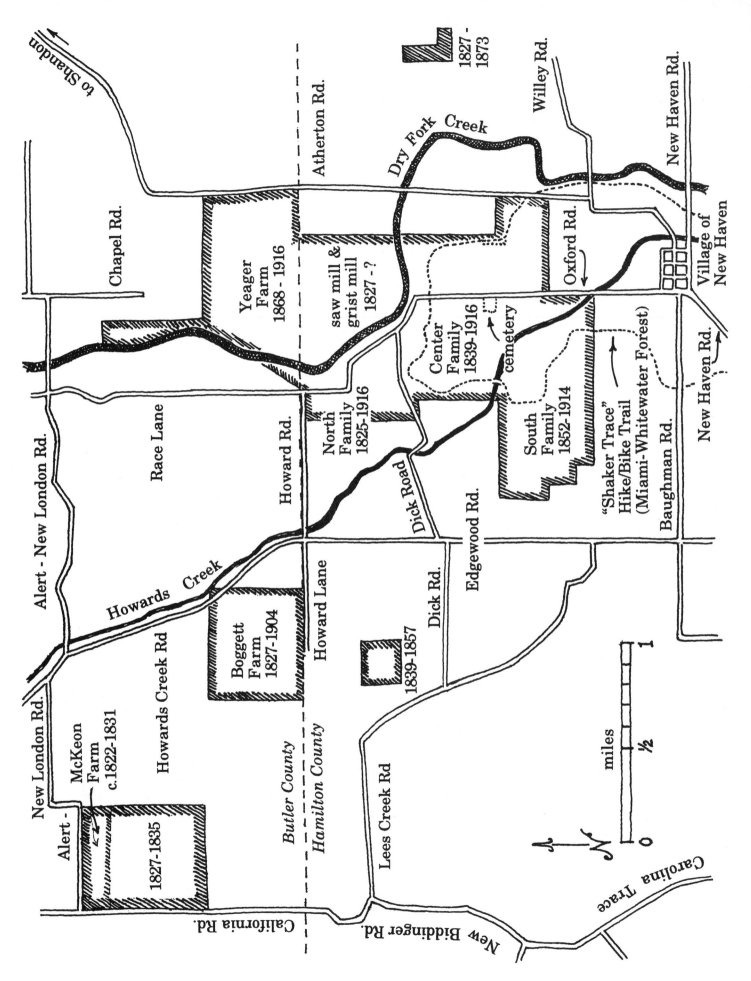

The White Water Shakers operated a grist mill, sawmill, and possibly a brewery. They raised broom corn and manufactured brooms...

Broom Shop at White Water

the Dry Fork commenced operations. That year membership swelled when West Union was dissolved.

In 1835 there were 42 females and 35 males, including children, in spite of defections during years just past.

Another group that added to the ranks of the White Water Shakers were followers of William Miller. He predicted the exact moment in April 1843 for Christ's Second Coming. People wound up their earthly affairs, dressed in ascension robes, and waited. Miller set another date six months later, but that final judgment day passed, too. His disappointed followers, the Millerites or Second Adventists, were courted by the Shakers who convinced the Millerites that the Shakers had already experienced the Second Coming in a spiritual sense.

At its peak with the conversion of the Millerites in 1846, White Water village comprised 706 acres in Hamilton County and 190 acres in Butler County on which 200 Believers in two families worked the large farm and engaged in a variety of industries. The Shakers would purchase additional land and establish a third family in the 1850s, and they remained a vibrant community into the 1880s when the long, slow decline began. The White

Water Shakers operated a grist mill, sawmill, and possibly a brewery. They raised broom corn and manufactured brooms, sold packaged garden seeds (grossing $5,704 in 1857),[2] and maintained large apple orchards for the sale of applesauce and cider. Other industries included sorghum molasses, honey, and preserved currents, grapes, and strawberries. The Shakers also raised silk worms for the manufacture of their own shawls, scarves, and handkerchiefs. In the final years of the community, the Believers were well known for raising fish in two Shaker-made ponds and for selling turkey eggs.

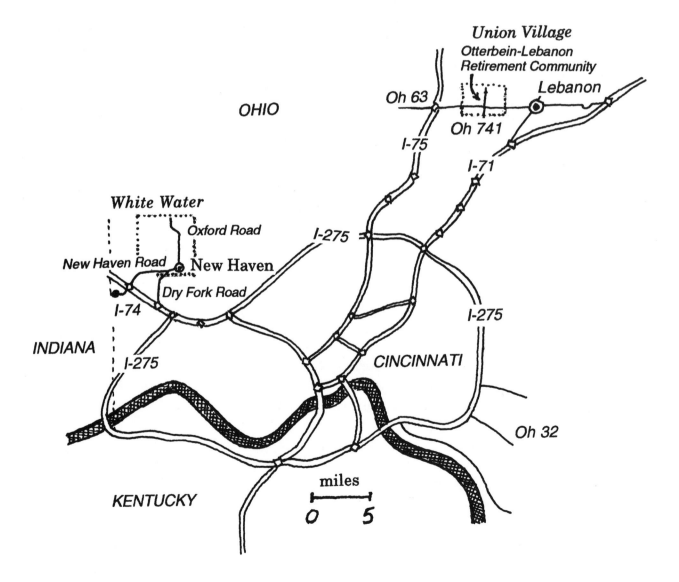

Land owned by the community over its 94 years of existence included 1,128 acres in Hamilton County, 664 acres in Butler County, and 972 acres in Clinton County—totaling 2,764 acres.

The Civil War affected the White Water community. For example, Morgan's Raiders, led by Col. John Hunt Morgan, a Confederate cavalry leader from Kentucky, came in April 1863. A mill worker warned the rest of the community of the approach of the Raiders and the Shakers quickly hid their horses.[3] Only two horses were stolen. The next day, however, 500 to 600 of the Union Army cavalry troops arrived. They were commanded by John S. Hobart, who demanded to see the hidden horses so that he could select the two best.

After 30 years of decline and a change in leadership, in 1911 the Union Village ministry decided to lease the South, Center, and North Family farms. The remaining Shakers resided in the Office until 1916, when the farms were sold. Land owned by the community over its 94 years of existence included 1,128 acres in Hamilton County, 664 acres in Butler County, and 972 acres in Clinton County—totaling 2,764 acres.[4] December 4, 1916, marked the final land sale and the departure of Elder Andrew Barrett and Eldress Mary Gass. Elder Barrett went to Hancock, the Shaker community near Pittsfield, Massachussetts. Eldress Mary Gass went to Mount Lebanon, New York, the leading Shaker community in the East. While the South and Center farms remained in agricultural use, the North Family land was subsequently divided and the brick Meeting House and Dwelling House passed to separate owners.

In 1991 the Hamilton County Park District purchased much of the remaining White Water buildings and land. The Park District owns 23 original Shaker-built or Shaker-used structures, including the 1827 two-story meetinghouse (the only extant brick Shaker meetinghouse), the 1832-33 North Family dwelling, a brick Trustee's Office with its 1855 date stone, a brick shop, a frame broom shop, and numerous barns and farm outbuildings. In all, this is the largest collection of Shaker buildings in Ohio and represents one of the most intact of all the Shaker villages.

The primary Shaker burying ground with more that 100 burials is just south of the Office. It is maintained by Crosby Township and is open to the public.

The Hamilton County Park District has completed a foot, bicycle, and equestrian trail—"Shaker Trace"—through its newly acquired Shaker land which you may follow. (See the White Water Shaker site map.) None of the Shaker buildings are open to the public at this time.

Richard Spence

...the 1827 two-story meetinghouse (is) the only extant brick Shaker meetinghouse...

White Water Center Family Dwelling

---

[1] J.P. MacLean, *Shakers of Ohio*, 236.

[2] Ibid., 257.

[3] Ibid., 263.

[4] Beth J. Parker Miller, 1988. Whitewater Architecture: A Study of Extant Shaker-Related Buildings on Whitewater-Owned Land in Southwest Ohio (Master's thesis, Wright State University, Dayton, Ohio), 108-149.

Chapter 17

North Union

Cuyahoga County, Ohio

Ralph Russell, a native of Windsor Locks, Connecticut, deserves credit for the founding of North Union, Ohio, "The Valley of God's Pleasure." In 1812, he moved to Warrensville Township, Cuyahoga County, with a group of 20 relatives who were led by his father, Jacob Russell. The difficult 600-mile journey was negotiated in a little more than two months. The Western Reserve land they entered became the nucleus of the North Union Shaker community.

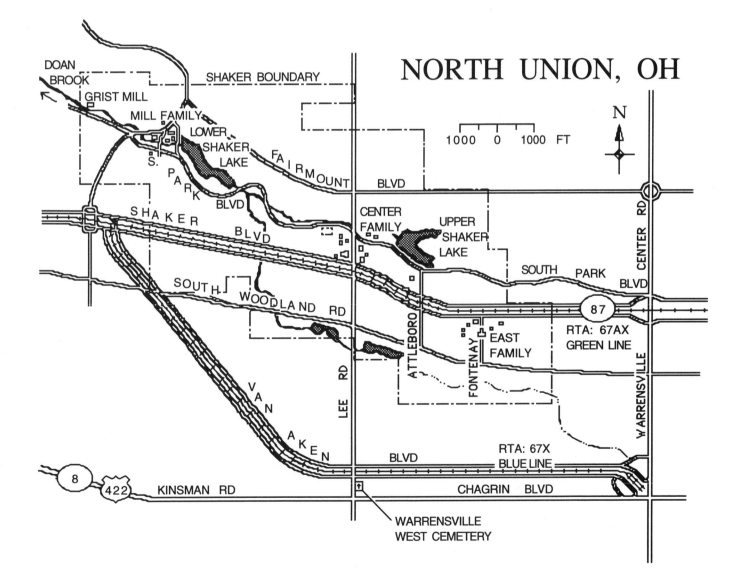

During the winter of 1820, Russell met James Darrow, whose brother, David, was an elder at Union Village. Ralph became interested in the Shaker religion. After the death of his father, Ralph traveled to Union Village. He intended to join the Shakers. Instead the elders instructed him to start a new community. When he returned home, Ralph shared his new-found faith with his wife, brothers, sisters, and neighbors. Elders Richard W. Pelham and James Hodge were dispatched from Union Village to help establish the work. On March 31, 1822, they held the first public meeting. "By February 1824, enough members had gathered at North Union to organize the Center Family in the cabins on the Lee Road-Shaker Boulevard property."[1]

A frame Center Family dwelling house, 30 feet by 40 feet and two stories high, was completed in May 1826. It was located on the west side of the present Lee Road, north of Shaker Boulevard. (Contrary to popular belief, Lee Road was not named in honor of Mother Ann Lee but rather for a local farmer, Elias Lee.)

The organization of North Union was completed in the fall of 1828 when a covenant was signed by 80 members. Many Russell family members were signers, but Ralph Russell and his wife, Laura, did not sign. They accepted $200 for their portion of North Union acreage and moved to Solon, Ohio, with their three children and widowed mother.

The community prospered. Brooms and buckets, dairy products, and produce all found a market in the expanding Cleveland area. In 1834, Eastern Shaker visitors told about one industry: "There are 2 looms in one room—& a great many green window curtains hang in one apartment, these they make for sale; they are made of wood splints & thread warp."[2]

An impressive five-story gristmill was built of Berea sandstone from the Shaker quarry in 1843. (It was blown up July 5, 1886, by its new owner, Cleveland City Councilman Charles Reader who wanted to sell the stone.) It was known for producing some of the best flour in Ohio. The Mill Family also operated a sawmill.

The Center Family operated a woolen mill built in 1854. Spinning, carding, and weaving took place in the building. Most of the wool was manufactured into stocking yarn. Silk worms were also cultivated for thread and cloth while flax was grown for linen production at North Union.

From 1822 to 1889 this community represented the Shaker spirit in the Cleveland area. By 1840 there were 100 members in the Center Family

From 1822 to 1889 this community represented
the Shaker spirit in the Cleveland area.

and 50 members each in the East Family and the Mill Family.[3] But that was the apex of membership. By 1870, there were 125 residents in the three families. In 1888 its long time leader, James Prescott, died. Within a year "on October 24, 1889, the North Union Society was dissolved; an auction was held to dispose of all the surplus chattels."[4] Twenty-seven of the remaining members moved either to Union Village or to Watervliet, Ohio.

Although no Shaker buildings remain in what is now known as Shaker Heights, one can visit Horseshoe Lake and the Lower Lake formed when the Shakers dammed Doan Brook which ran through the center of the slightly rolling narrow valley. The gravesite of Jacob Russell, a Revolutionary War veteran, is located across from the Shaker Historical Museum on South Park Boulevard. On display in the North Union Gallery of the Museum is a permanent exhibit of furniture and artifacts once used by the North Union Shakers. The Museum's Nord Library includes the North Union funeral hymns and burial record book; Brother James Prescott's Village Harmony hymnal which he carried from New England; and the Pilot Family Bible belonging to a Shaker family from Little Falls, New York.

Other reminders of the Shakers are a marker on Fontenay Road for the site of the East Family dwelling house and two stone gateposts on the northeast corner of Lee Road and Shaker Boulevard, marking the site of the Shaker Meeting House. The Warrensville West Cemetery on Lee Road near

Center Family North Union

Details of Center Family

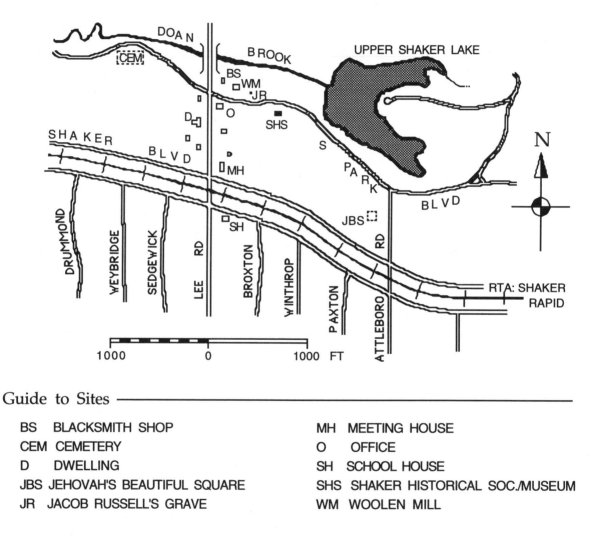

Guide to Sites

BS   BLACKSMITH SHOP
CEM   CEMETERY
D   DWELLING
JBS   JEHOVAH'S BEAUTIFUL SQUARE
JR   JACOB RUSSELL'S GRAVE

MH   MEETING HOUSE
O   OFFICE
SH   SCHOOL HOUSE
SHS   SHAKER HISTORICAL SOC./MUSEUM
WM   WOOLEN MILL

Chagrin Boulevard contains the common burial plot where the Shakers were reinterred in 1909 by the Van Sweringen brothers' land development company. They had purchased the 1,366 acres of North Union land to begin the garden-city suburb, first known as "Shaker Village," now called Shaker Heights.

Cathie Winans
Rose Mary Lawson

Planning Your Visit to North Union

   A visit to the Shaker Historical Society, 16740 South Park Boulevard, Shaker Heights, 44120, will furnish a noteworthy perspective on the heritage of North Union. The museum is located in one of the first garden-city suburbs, Shaker Heights, which followed the Shakers' ownership of the land. Museum hours are Tuesday through Friday, 2 P.M. to 5 P.M., Sunday, 2 P.M. to 5 P.M. Closed holidays. The Spirit Tree Museum Shop, carrying Shaker reproductions, books, miniatures, CDs and tapes about the Shakers, is open during museum hours. The Elizabeth Nord Library is open Tuesday through

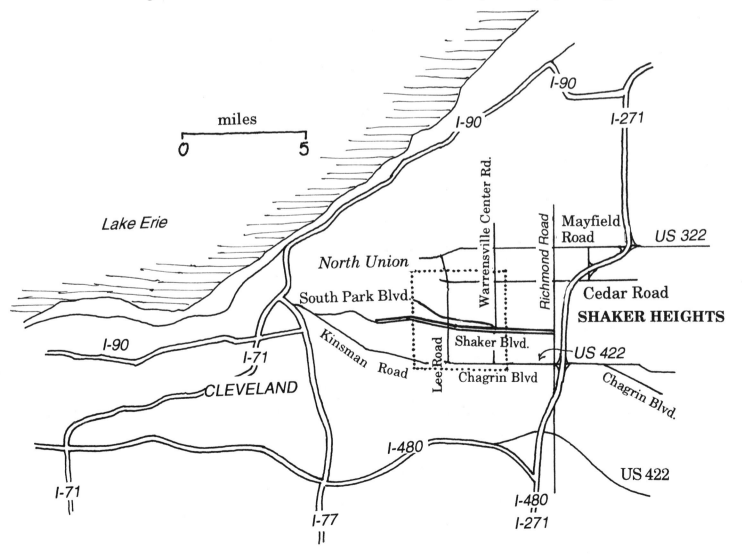

Friday, 2 P.M. to 5 P.M. Special arrangements may be made for group tours and meetings. Phone: (216) 921-1201. The museum web site may be visited, too: http://www.cwru.edu/orgs/shakhist/shaker.htm

To explore some nearby Shaker land, visit the Shaker Lakes Regional Nature Center at 2600 South Park Boulevard, Shaker Heights. A part of the Doan Brook watershed, the center has hiking trails leading to six natural habitats and an accessible marsh boardwalk. The Nature Center building with offices, community meeting rooms, and the Duck Pond Gift Shop is open Monday through Saturday from 9 A.M. to 5 P.M. and Sunday from 1 P.M. to 5 P.M. Closed on holidays. Phone: (216) 321-5935.

Closer to downtown Cleveland, the Western Reserve Historical Society, 10825 East Boulevard, University Circle, offers insights into North Union history as well as one of the finest collections of Shaker books and manuscripts in its library. Hours are Monday through Saturday, 10 A.M. to 5 P.M., Sunday, NOON to 5 P.M. Closed on holidays. The library is open Tuesday through Saturday, 9 A.M. to 5 P.M., also Wednesday evenings, 5 P.M. to 9 P.M. Phone: (216) 721-5722.

[1] Mary Lou Conlin, *The North Union Story* (Shaker Heights, Ohio: Shaker Historical Society, 1961; reprint, 1975), 2

[2] *Journal of Issac Newton Youngs*, Vol. 1, June 18, 1834, Shaker Museum and Library, Old Chatham, New York.

[3] J .P. MacLean, *Shakers of Ohio*, 125.

[4] Carolyn B. Piercy, *The Valley of God's Pleasure* (New York: Stratford House Press, 1951), 240.

Chapter 18

Expanding Land Holdings
and the Underground Railroad

During the 1850s many Shaker communities acquired property at some distance from their primary sites. Although there are many reasons why this surge of land ownership might have taken place, one possibility which has not been explored is that the Shakers were part of the Underground Railroad. The urgent secrecy of the enterprise and perhaps its intentional omission in the Shaker journals make it difficult to prove this possibility, however. The timing and location of the acquisitions support this thesis.

Union Village, a stop on the Underground Railroad, began purchasing land in Clinton County, Ohio, late in 1856 from a man known as "a staunch Abolitionist." Then White Water acquired two nearby tracts in April 1857. In August of that same year, Union Village purchased another farm along the Kankakee River in northern Indiana, an area where the river was utilized to transport slaves toward Canada.

Daniel Brainard acquired two small lots in Henry County, Ohio, along the Maumee River in 1824 before joining the Watervliet, New York, Shaker community in 1827. In 1857 he sold both tracts for one dollar to the Watervliet Shakers. Henry County families have an oral tradition linking their families and the Shakers in their area with the Underground Railroad along the Maumee River and the Miami and Erie Canal.

In April 1859, New Lebanon, New York, joined this program of outreach, purchasing a farm along the St. Joseph River in Berrien County, Michigan. The story that the barn, enlarged by the Shakers, sheltered escaped slaves circulates in that county.

The Shakers at Watervliet, New York, owned land in Illinois given to them by Reuben Treadway in the late 1820s or early 1830s. The farm was located near the community of Hudson in McLean County, southwest of Chicago. After looking over the property in 1855, the Shakers had a house and barn built there, then hired a tenant farmer to run the farm.[1] Underground Railroad paths crossed Illinois from Missouri and other states, focusing on Chicago and from there to Canada via the Great Lakes .

The Underground Railroad was in existence as early as 1815,[2] but its activity greatly increased after the passage of the Fugitive Slave Law in 1850. That law made it possible for slave hunters to come into free states and to take blacks back into slavery. The act placed the full power of federal law

Religious communities played a significant role
in transporting slaves northward.

enforcement behind the apprehension of slave runaways. The Underground Railroad was dangerous business and those who cooperated in the enterprise would not share information about their involvement with others. Participants might know only the next stop north, about 20 miles away. Then they would not be able to answer too many questions. Severe fines and even imprisonment were the penalty if one were caught by the authorities. The communities of free blacks were the primary source of assistance to escaping slaves, but others also provided "safe houses."

Religious communities played a significant role in transporting slaves northward. John Rankin of Ripley, Ohio, kept twinkling lights in the windows of his hilltop home overlooking the Ohio River, guiding many slaves in their eventual escape to Canada. This Presbyterian minister was fined and imprisoned for his activities.

S.W. Gilliland's home in Brown County was on the path northward beyond Ripley. He was the minister for the Red Oak Presbyterian Church, having taken John Dunlavy's place after the latter became a Shaker.[3] Wesleyan Methodists, Presbyterians, and especially the Quakers were the known driving forces in the Underground Railroad in Ohio and other states as well. Levi Coffin, called the president of the Underground Railroad, used his home in Fountain City, Indiana, to expedite the movement of slaves from Cincinnati to Lake Michigan. Coffin was a Quaker.[4]

Ohio, Indiana, Illinois, and Michigan were all admitted to statehood as "free states." The Ohio River formed a circuitous and undulating path between free and slave states. It seems likely that the Shakers played some role in the network of routes that developed north of this river which took slaves to Great Lakes ports or from Michigan via Detroit or Port Huron directly into Canada—and freedom.

---

[1] Letter to the author from Elizabeth Shaver, March 16, 1996.

[2] Charles L. Blockson, *The Underground Railroad* (New York: Prentice Hall Press, 1987), 206.

[3] Mary Harrison Games, *The Underground Railroad in Ohio* (s.l., ca. 1937), 62; John Dunlavy advocated the immediate abolition of slavery when he preached in Brown County from 1790 to 1805. William Birney, *James G. Birney and His Times* (New York: D. Appleton and Co., 1890), 399, 432.

[4] Blockson, 203.

Chapter 19

Union Village and White Water Acquisitions

in Clinton County, Ohio and Farther Afield

There is a brooding quality to Oliver Hampton's writing in a Union Village journal during 1856. In addition to the chronicle of events and the comings and goings of people, he worried "aloud" about some of his deep concerns and fears. A few weeks before the Union Village Shakers purchased land in Clinton County, he wrote, "I would to God I could feel some easier on some particular subjects, but the ministry are away most of the time and I can say nothing to any body else that would in the least relieve my feelings." He reflected about those who suffered from "an accusing conscience. . .others slowly devoured by the green eyed monster jealousy whose vengeance never sleeps. . .some are tortur'd with the accurs'd slave-whip till life is crushed out." Hampton often contemplated the need to trust in Divine Providence.[1] Perhaps his concern stemmed from Shaker involvement in the illegal activities of the Underground Railroad.

Two farms in Jefferson Township, Clinton County, totaling 1,572 acres were purchased in December 1856 by the Union Village Shakers from Robert G. Corwin, described as "a staunch Abolitionist of Lebanon." Corwin's family owned, but did not occupy, a farm near Greentree (at the

Office at White Water

corner of Greentree Road and Route 741 near the northern boundary of Union Village). Two black women were allowed to use this farm to conceal fugitive slaves as they passed through the Lebanon area. Their next stop was Springboro, along the same road as Union Village, reputedly another link in the informally organized Underground Railroad, according to Job Mullin of Springboro.[2]

The Union Village land purchases in Clinton County were south of the town of Martinsville, a Quaker stronghold. Here the principal "safe house" was the home of Christopher C. Betts, a wealthy Quaker.[3] One path for escaping slaves swept northward from Ripley, went through Red Oak, Sardinia, Lynchburg, and to Martinsville. The other route extended

Underground Railroad Routes
to Martinsville

100

...both farms could have been part of the network of paths and dirt roads...known collectively as the Underground Railroad.

northeastwardly from New Richmond and Moscow along the Ohio River and went directly to Martinsville. Both routes went on to Wilmington and from there in various directions.

A branch of the East Fork of the Little Miami River makes a sweep around the southeastern corner of the larger Shaker farm and could have served as a guide for slaves escaping toward Martinsville. The Cincinnati and Hillsboro Railroad crossed the other farm.[4] Although no known Shaker manuscripts confirm it, both farms could have been part of the network of paths and dirt roads through little traveled areas; river and stream crossings; and boats, trains and wagons known collectively as the Underground Railroad.

Apparently the original intention of the Union Village Shakers was to start another community in Clinton County. Hopes were high as five brethren and several sisters moved there for a time. Apple, peach, cherry, and pear trees were planted in the expectation of a long stay. Late in 1857 the Shakers made an intensive effort to meet their Clinton County neighbors by visiting in homes, participating in local seances (communicating one evening with Union Village brothers Daniel Staggs, Gabriel Hattan, and John Webster, all of whom had died in recent years), attending a quarterly meeting of the Martinsville Quakers, and holding a Shaker meeting at Westboro. They toured a nearby Catholic academy in Brown County. These contacts with farm neighbors and those who were members of established churches did not produce any converts. The pioneers soon returned to Union Village.[5]

Trustee Ithamar Johnson was in charge of the farms; however he was often needed in both Union Village and Clinton County. One spring it was reported that the Clinton cattle were suffering from eating May apples, the sheep were starving and vulnerable to dog attacks, the land was flooded, and the purchase overall was "rather a dull figure."[6] Yet "Clinton Valley" or "Clinton Grove," as the Shakers called it, was productive, supplying not only pasturage but also broom corn, cooper staves, wagon spokes, hay, hazel nuts, wild berries and herbs.

In 1857 the White Water Shakers also purchased two Clinton County farms in neighboring Clark Township for cattle pasturage with a total of 972 acres. The farms were directly south of Martinsville, not far from the Union Village farms purchased from Corwin.

By 1862 some of the Clinton Valley land was rented out. In early

101

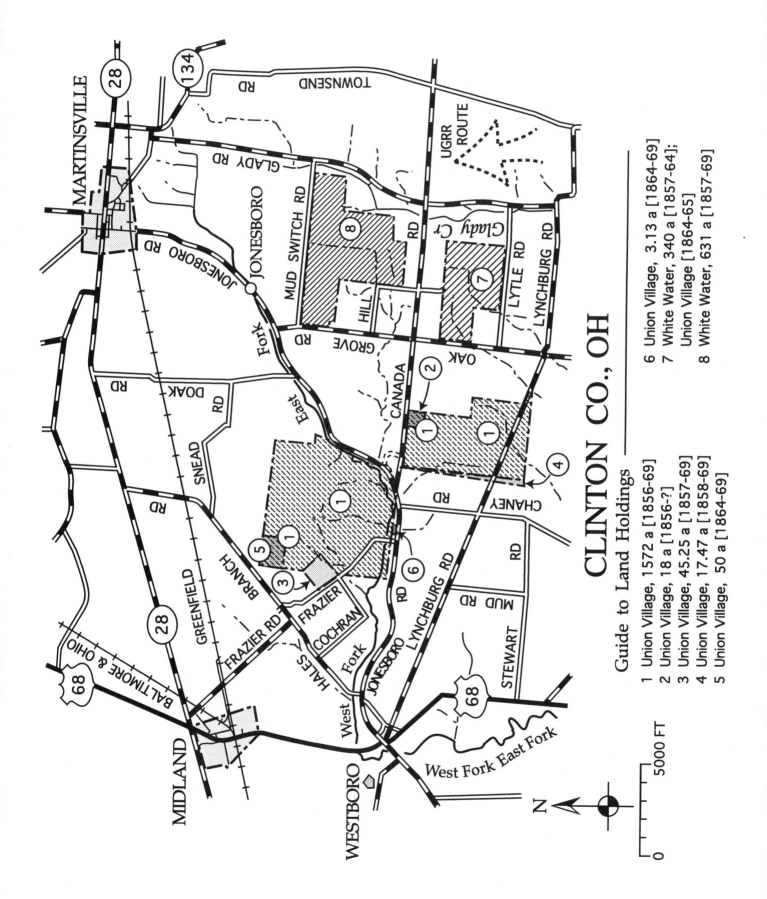

CLINTON CO., OH

Guide to Land Holdings

1 Union Village, 1572 a [1856-69]
2 Union Village, 18 a [1856-?]
3 Union Village, 45.25 a [1857-69]
4 Union Village, 17.47 a [1858-69]
5 Union Village, 50 a [1864-69]

6 Union Village, 3.13 a [1864-69]
7 White Water, 340 a [1857-64];
  Union Village [1864-65]
8 White Water, 631 a [1857-69]

1864 Union Village purchased White Water's tract of 340 acres for $5,400, then sold it in December 1865 for $4,000. William Reynolds explained the situation: "Ithamar [Johnson] is in a strait for money just now and this will clear him off once more. He says we own yet about 1,600 acres in that farm and. . .in my opinion we had better sell for whatever we can get for it."[7] Perhaps the fact that the Civil War was over was an unwritten part of the explanation. Both Union Village and White Water sold the balance of their Clinton County land in 1869.

Farther afield, Union Village acquired a 480-acre farm in LaPorte County, Indiana, on the Kankakee River in August 1857. Twelve head of cattle were sold for $5,400 to purchase the land. In November, however, when a Shaker next visited the northern Indiana purchase, the land was all under water. This may have seemed like a poor investment for a farm, but if taken in the context of usefulness for the Underground Railroad, its significance changes. Runaway slaves followed a path across Indiana which took them

> to a point near Lake Michigan either in Lake, Porter or LaPorte Counties. [All these counties have the Kankakee River within their bounds.] Here there was a place in each county where they were secreted and smuggled on board a lumber bark that the anti-slavery people owned and that was manned by an anti-slavery crew. This boat was very unpretentious to look at but was built for strength and speed. Anyone not acquainted would think the boat would not dare venture five miles from shore. The boat cruised along the shore landing at different points in the three counties, loading and unloading freight as was offered them but carrying no passengers. The negroes were kept secreted in the holds until a number were gathered together and then taken along the Michigan shore on up into Canada.[8]

The Union Village journals also refer to land in Canada:

June 23, 1857. H. L. Eades starts for Canada on business & returned the 26th Inst.

November 17, 1863. Elder Cephas to Canada West his business is Land.

November 1, 1864. P[eter] Boyd went to Canada to settle some property in lands. [9]

Union Village, "whose second convert was Anna Middleton, a slave, who was received just as cordially as though she had been white and free,"[10] reportedly had a network of tunnels joining some of its buildings[11] as well as a network of farms which may well have served to transport slaves to freedom on invisible rails through Ohio and Indiana and ultimately into Canada.

[1] *Church Journal Kept by Oliver C. Hampton* (1856-1859), WRHS V:B-246, December 18, 1856.

[2] Games, *Underground Railroad in Ohio*, 54; letter from W.H. Newport to W.H. Siebert, September 16, 1895. Siebert collection, Ohio Historical Society.
 Newport wrote for his father-in-law, Job Mullin:
   "Item 1st The UGRR was to assist Fugitives or Slaves out of bondage by forming Stations thrue this State so as to get them through to Canada. I cannot give but 3 names of Stations: Union or Shaker Vilage, Waynesville & Springboro.
   "Item 2nd The most active time to my knolage was from 1816 to 1830."

[3] Harry C. Ertel, "The Underground Railroad—A Part of Clinton County's History" (lecture at the Springfield Meeting House for the DAR, October 30, 1989).

[4] Robert G. Corwin who sold the Union Village Shakers their land wrote to Wilbur H. Siebert on September 11, 1895, "An arrangement was made with the railroads running from Cincinnati to Sandusky to carry fugitives in their baggage cars." Siebert collection, Ohio Historical Society.

[5] Sharon L. Edwards, "Union Village Land Holdings: Clinton County, Kankakee." Chapter 3 of the book, *Life at Union Village: Shaker Agriculture and Industry 1805-1870* (forthcoming); Hampton, *Church Journal*, October 27-November 3, 1857.

[6] *Daily Record of Events of the Church Family*, WRHS V:B-231, May 19, 1861.

[7] *Church Journal of Current Events at Union Village Kept by William Reynolds*, WRHS V:B-256, December 22, 1865.

[8] William M. Cockrum, *History of the Underground Railroad* (New York: Negro Universities Press, 1915, Reprinted, 1969), 18.

[9] *Daily Record of Events of the Church Family*, WRHS V:B-230, 336; *Church Journal of Current Events at Union Village Kept by William Reynolds*, WRHS V:B-255, 151 and WRHS V:B-256, 16.

[10] MacLean, *Shakers of Ohio*, 63.

[11] Edwina Essex, "Two 'Underground' Routes Led Into Lebanon," *The Western Star*, Lebanon, Ohio, April 11, 1973.

Chapter 20

Land in Henry County, Ohio

Daniel Brainard was one of the first to purchase land by patent in Henry County, in northwestern Ohio, in 1824. The area, flattened by the thrust of the glacier, was known as the Black Swamp and was the last part of Ohio to be settled.

Southwestern Ohio was opened to European settlement after the signing of the Treaty of Greenville in 1795, but northwestern Ohio remained under Ottawa Indian control. As a reward for remaining neutral in the War of 1812, the Ottawas were granted additional reservations along the Maumee River. It was pressure from the state of Indiana to complete the Wabash and Erie Canal along the Maumee River that led to treaties for Indian removal. This removal to Kansas was not completed until 1839.[1]

Listed in the Henry County deeds as a resident of Maumee, a community adjacent to Toledo, Brainard purchased a 12.5 acre tract along the Maumee River across from the town of Florida in Flatrock Township as well as 3.9 acres and Sargeant Island's 6 acres (no deed issued) in Napoleon Township.[2] The Miami and Erie Canal, completed in Henry County in 1842, crossed part of Brainard's 9.9-acre site.

Brainard may have invested in the land to profit from the location of the canal. Or he may have wanted to help the Ottawa Indians during the protracted negotiations before their removal. It may also have been his desire to assist with Underground Railroad activities. The area along the Maumee River in northwestern Ohio is described by Wilbur H. Siebert as "probably the oldest [part of the Underground Railroad] in Ohio," with its period of greatest activity from the early 1820s to 1840.[3] Both pieces of land were subsequently sold by Brainard to "Chauncey Miller and Chauncey Copley, Trustees of the United Society of People Called Shakers of the Society at Watervliet within the County of Albany in the State of New York" on April 1, 1857, for one dollar.

As a Shaker, Brainard lived first at New Lebanon where he was described as a "horticulturist." Perhaps he became associated with the Shakers about the time he purchased the Henry County land. On March 7, 1827, he joined the South Family at Watervliet, New York, then moved the following year to the West Family. In August 1847 Copley, a Church Family trustee at Watervliet, and Brainard traveled to Ohio "to see to & settle some business relative to Daniel's possessions near the Maumee River."[4]

16

In August 1847 Copley, a Church Family trustee at Watervliet, and Brainard traveled to Ohio "to see to & settle some business relative to Daniel's possessions near the Maumee River.

Records of the Tanner family of Henry County describe the 9.9-acre tract:

> *At one time there was a small building, kind of across from Round Bottom, that had been used for a meeting house by some kind of religious group. Their bell ringing could be heard, if the wind was right, for a long distance and house wives served their noon meal by that bell. The log building sat quite close to the river. The group moved when the canal came through and took part of their land . . . .[They] made a lot of noise when at worship.[5]*

An archaeological dig organized by Richard M. Helwig in 1984 found this 12.5-acre tract contained a log barn separated by a deep ravine from a two-story log house. Between the house and the barn along the ravine a forge site was found.[6]

Tubbs family records provide more information about this property. Their oral tradition indicates that the first structure on the 12.5-acre site was a temporary cabin built between 1835 and 1845. It may have been built by Brainard or a squatter. This building of rough-hewn logs was located along the road on the south side of the ravine. A one-story building, its loft was accessible by a ladder. One door was centered on the long side of the house facing the road while another door faced the ravine.

A two-story log house, located near the road on the north side of the ravine, was built around 1848. Measuring about 28 feet by 16 feet, it had two rooms downstairs, two rooms up. A cooking area was added to the west side of the house. The interior walls were plastered and a fireplace had a stone hearth with a brick chimney. The building began to deteriorate in the 1950s. Logs and clapboards were removed over the years, and ultimately the structure collapsed and rotted.[7] Large foundation stones from the house are still visible near the road.

After the second house was built, the temporary cabin served as a small barn. Its attic provided a place where slaves were hidden overnight or no longer than two days. A trapdoor to the attic could be bolted from the attic side. Then a code word let the occupants know that it was all right to slide the bolt to open the trapdoor. The Shakers seemed to escape investigation as an Underground Railroad stop.

A larger barn was added to the property in about 1859 in the same position as the first cabin, which was moved 30 to 40 feet directly behind the

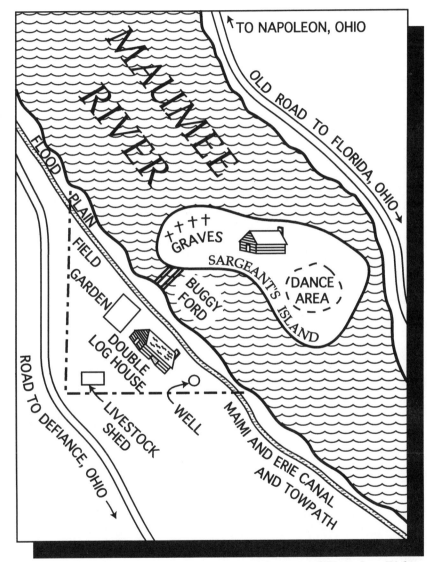

courtesy of Genevieve Eicher

Sketch (not to scale) of 3.9 acres of Shaker land in the flood plain and 6.0 acres on Sargeant's Island in Napoleon Township, Henry County, Ohio. Information given to Alice Motter by her parents, Charles and Charlotte Tubbs, who lived about eight miles from the Shakers.

...the location of the site, plus the maze of ravines and gullies on the river side of the [land] made it an ideal station site on the Underground Railroad.

barn. It then served as a storage shed. Foundation stones indicate the barn was 28 feet by 25 feet. Hinges and hasps located in the dig suggest there were three doors to the barn. A corn crib, 7 feet by 12 feet and located along the south side of the barn, may have been added in 1861.[8] The deteriorating barn was used for fire practice in the 1960s.

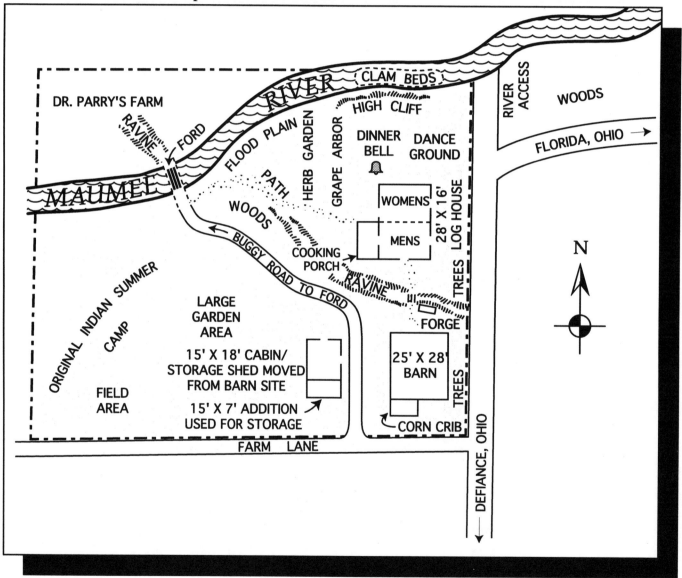

courtesy of Genevieve Eicher

Sketch (not to scale) of 12.5 acres of Shaker land near Florida, Ohio, in Flatrock Township, Henry County, Ohio. Information told to Alice Motter by her parents, Charles and Charlotte Tubbs.

The wooded area around the house and barn provided enough cover that activities in the ravine might not be observed from the road. The ravine ended at the south bank of the Maumee River where there were shallows, making it possible to wade across the river in the summer.

Sometimes neighbors were invited to gather, at the invitation of the Shakers, to share religious services at this 12.5-acre site. The parts of the day remembered by the guests were the singing and the dancing. When the ground was soaked after heavy rains, the Shakers might sing and dance on the trail going past their farm.[9]

As Helwig studied the community of Florida and the Shaker presence in the area, his conclusion was that

> the primary reason for the Shakers establishing their colony on Brainard lands was. . .the location of the site, plus the maze of ravines and gullies on the river side of the [land] made it an ideal station site on the Underground Railroad. In addition, a narrow shallow walkway led from the mouth of these ravines across the Maumee to Dr. [Gibbons] Parry's house. . . .Dr Parry. . .operated . . .[a station] on the Underground Railroad. It is highly probable that the Shaker settlement was also a station on the Underground Railroad.[10]

Records of the Tubbs family, also operating a "safe house" close to Dr. Parry, tell the following story about a black woman who arrived at the Shakers' location on the south bank of the river on her way to freedom. She had never before seen ice and had no fear of its breaking up. The Shaker family on the south bank forgot to warn her to be careful. She fell through the ice, but managed to get herself out of the river and up to the Parry's back door. Dr. Parry quickly moved her on to the Tubbs' home with the excuse that Mrs. Tubbs was very, very sick and he had to get there as soon as possible. Before the Tubbs family could move her to the next stop, their visitor became very ill with a high fever and lost consciousness.

It was necessary for Dr. Parry to travel to the Tubbs' home just about every day until the woman was able to be moved. The patient was sedated to keep her quiet. Charles Tubbs' wife, Lucy, knew the dangers of hiding slaves, so she kept a wary eye for people coming to her house. As soon as she saw a horse and buggy, or a team and wagon coming, she put her night gown over her day clothing, jumped into bed, and pretended to be quite ill. Lucy was relieved when their black guest could be moved and told everyone her

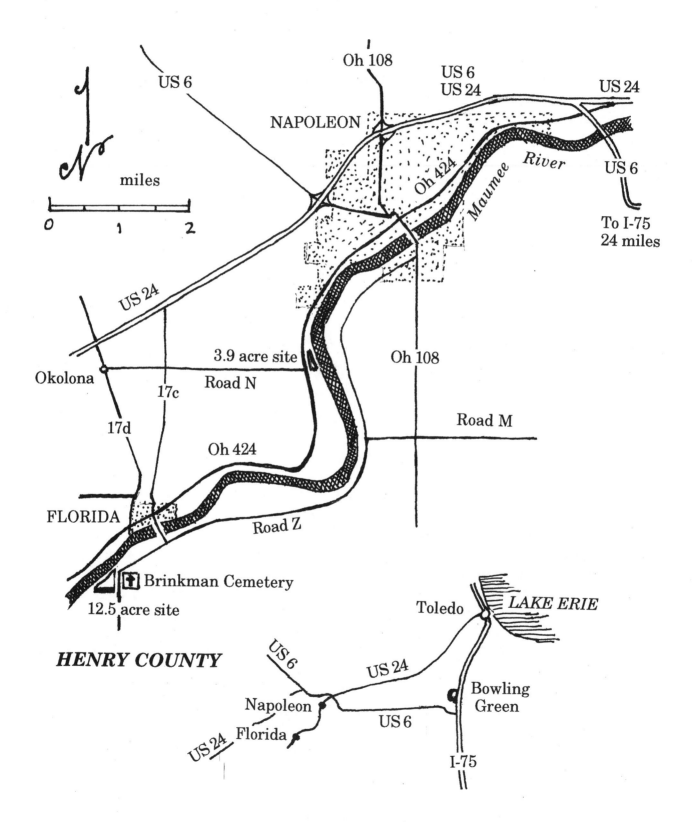

miles

0   1   2

US 6

Oh 108

US 6
US 24

US 24

NAPOLEON

Oh 424

Maumee River

US 6

To I-75
24 miles

US 24

3.9 acre site

Okolona

17c

Road N

Oh 108

Road M

17d

Oh 424

FLORIDA

Road Z

Brinkman Cemetery

12.5 acre site

HENRY COUNTY

US 6

Toledo

LAKE ERIE

US 24

Napoleon

US 24

Florida

Bowling
Green

US 6

I-75

"miracle recovery" came from Dr. Parry's care and a new medicine he administered.[11]

With an untutored hand Ann Buckingham noted in a Watervliet journal on July 16, 1874, that Daniel Brainard "passed to Spirit land last night near 12 he has been a very hard working Brother ever since he came to believers he is 82 & worked on two Staffs and kept a splendid garden he eat breakfast as usual & at midnight was no more."[12] The two pieces of land in Henry County sold on September 1, 1874, to Dr. Gibbons Parry.

[1] Randolph C. Downes, *Canal Days*, Lucas County Historical Series, Vol. II (Toledo: Historical Society of Northwestern Ohio, 1949), 11-55.

[2] In the early days of the settlement of northwestern Ohio, islands were often claimed by squatters. No deeds were issued for islands, but their ownership went with nearby land until 1895 when the federal government sold them to the State of Ohio. Then the county recorders filed the deeds in their jurisdictions and the islands were sold at auction. The last deed for Sargeant Island was recorded in 1949; the island has disappeared completely since then. Research provided by Genevieve Eicher in an unpublished manuscript, "Islands in the Maumee River, Henry County, Ohio," March 1978.

[3] Wilbur H. Siebert, an Ohio State University professor who indefatigably collected information about the Underground Railroad, sketched the Miami and Erie Canal from Cincinnati to Toledo as a path for slaves on their northward journey. He indicated that the towpath of the final northern 80 miles of this canal also brought "wayfarers" from northeastern Indiana who made stops at scattered stations. Siebert, *Mysteries of Ohio's Underground Railroad* (Columbus: Long's College Book Co., 1951), 243. See also Siebert, "The Underground Railroad in Ohio," *Ohio Archaeological and Historical Quarterly* 4 (1895): 60-61.

[4] *Daily Journal of the First Order or Church Family*, Watervliet, NY. WRHS, V:B-321, August 9, 1847. Information about Daniel Brainard's life with the Watervliet Shakers provided by Elizabeth Shaver in a letter to the author, April 15, 1996.

[5] Genevieve Eicher, "Notes from an interview with Augustus Motter and his daughter, Genevieve," 1938.

[6] Richard M. Helwig, *Ohio Ghost Towns, No. 11: Henry County*, (Galena, Ohio: The Center for Ghost Town Research in Ohio, 1988), 37.

[7] Richard M. Helwig, *The History of Flatrock Township and Florida, Henry County, Ohio*, for The Snaketown/Florida Archaeological & Historical Project funded in part by the Ohio Humanities Council, "Summary and Conclusions" (Typescript research by Genevieve Eicher, 1984) s.l., s.a.

[8] Letter to the author from Genevieve Eicher, April 28, 1997.

[9] Letter to the author from Genevieve Eicher, March 23, 1997.

[10] Ibid.

[11] Helwig, *The History of Flatrock Township and Florida*, 178.

[12] *Ann Buckingham Journal*, July 16, 1874. New York State Museum file SC-20330, Box 9, Book 24.

Chapter 21

The Shaker Farm at Berrien Springs

Berrien County, Michigan

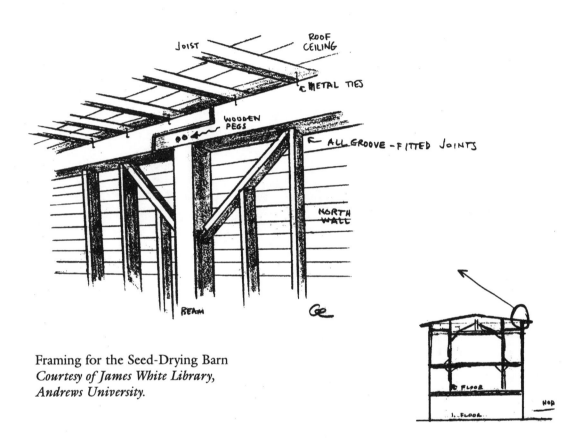

Framing for the Seed-Drying Barn
*Courtesy of James White Library,
Andrews University.*

At the same time the North Family at New Lebanon, New York, was excavating the foundation for its massive stone barn in 1859, it was also expanding its agrarian base to include a 350-acre farm on the rolling lands of Berrien County, Michigan. Described by the Shakers as "good land," heavily timbered in Berrien Springs,[1] the farm was close to the St. Joseph River in the southwestern corner of the state, not far from Lake Michigan. They paid $12,250 for the land.

The house on the property, located on a high bluff with a view of the river, was built by George Kimmel in 1832. Kimmel had come from Somerset County, Pennsylvania, and wanted a home to remind him of his eastern roots. He was among the first settlers in Oronoko Township, Berrien County, and with three daughters of marriageable age, his home became a center for hospitality in the area.

The 250-acre flood plain, owned by Andrews University, still produces a good corn crop.

Prior to his death in 1848, Kimmel had divided his large 2,000-acre farm into 400-acre lots. His son, George, received the 400 acres with the homestead. On April 8, 1859, the latter sold 350 acres of his farm including the homestead to the Shakers. The farm produced different kinds of seeds, grains, and grapes. The Shakers did not alter the house, but enlarged the barn and built a huge frame three-story structure behind it in which they dried and stored seeds. This building, erected shortly after the Civil War, was filled from top to bottom with rows of shelves for seed drying.[2]

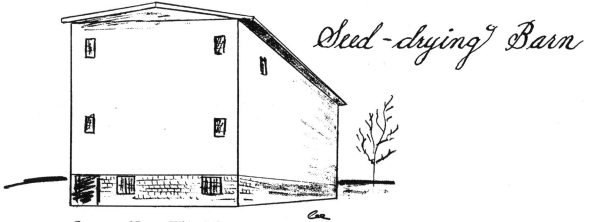

Seed-drying Barn

Courtesy of James White Library, Andrews University.

A story circulates in Berrien County that the Shaker Farm was used as a hiding place for fugitive slaves. M. O. Collins, who purchased the farm in the 1920s, said that the barn was built in the shape of a box car with a false floor that left a space of about four feet underneath. He said that the Shakers hid fugitives in this space. The nearby St. Joseph River site may have served as a northward path for the Underground Railroad as well.[3]

Abijah Estes was the first manager of the Berrien Springs farm. A Michigan native who became a Shaker at the North Family at New Lebanon in 1858, he managed the Michigan farm until he left the Shakers in the spring of 1860. The supervision of the farm operation passed to John Estes, a non-Shaker. When he died in 1862, his wife, Elizabeth, and their two young children, Peter and Frank, went to the North Family at New Lebanon, but left after just a month.

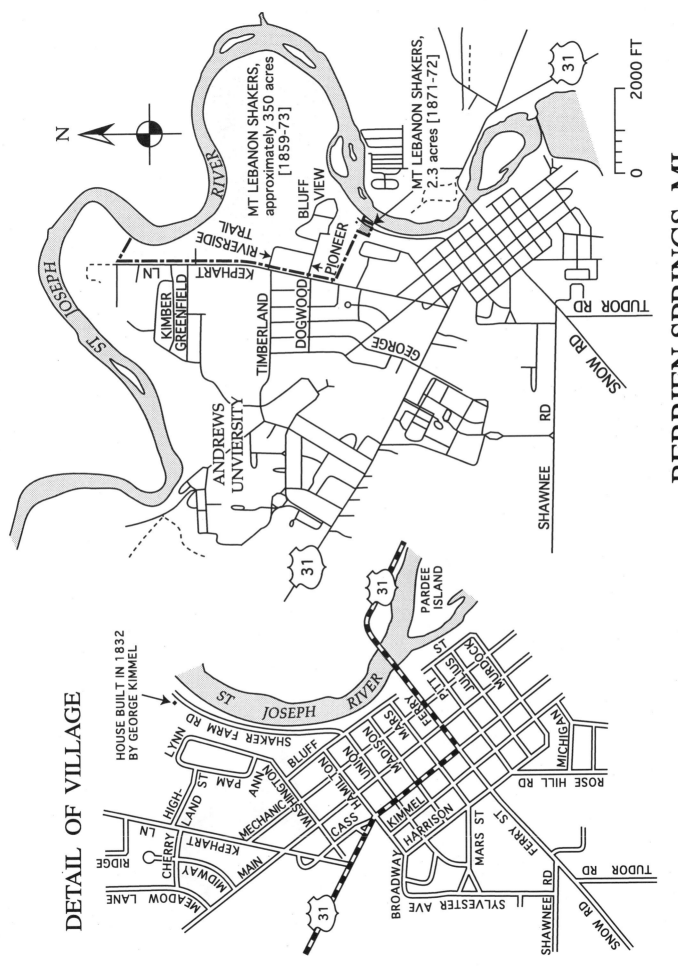

BERRIEN SPRINGS, MI

MT LEBANON SHAKERS, approximately 350 acres [1859-73]

MT LEBANON SHAKERS, 2.3 acres [1871-72]

N

2000 FT

0

BLUFF VIEW

RIVERSIDE TRAIL

PIONEER

KEPHART

ST JOSEPH RIVER

KIMBER

GREENFIELD

TIMBERLAND

DOGWOOD

GEORGE

ANDREWS UNVIERSITY

TUDOR RD

SNOW RD

SHAWNEE RD

31

31

PARDEE ISLAND

DETAIL OF VILLAGE

HOUSE BUILT IN 1832 BY GEORGE KIMMEL

ST JOSEPH RIVER

SHAKER FARM RD

RIDGE LN

CHERRY

HIGH-LAND ST

LYNN

PAM

ANN

MECHANIC

WASHINGTON

BLUFF

MEADOW LANE

MIDWAY

KEPHART

MAIN

UNION

HAMILTON

CASS

MADISON

MARS

FERRY ST

PITT

JULIUS

MURDOCK

ST

MICHIGAN

ROSE HILL RD

KIMMEL

HARRISON

BROADWAY

SYLVESTER AVE

MARS ST

FERRY ST

SHAWNEE RD

SYLVESTER RD

TUDOR RD

SNOW RD

31

31

115

An 1860 schedule of agricultural production for Berrien County indicates that on the 350-acre Shaker farm 181 acres were improved, 169 acres, unimproved. The livestock tally included nine horses, six milch (giving milk) cows, two working oxen, 27 other cattle, and 13 swine. The farm produced 750 bushels of wheat, 800 bushels of Indian corn, 40 bushels of oats, 40 bushels of Irish potatoes, 30 tons of hay as well as 600 pounds of butter.[4]

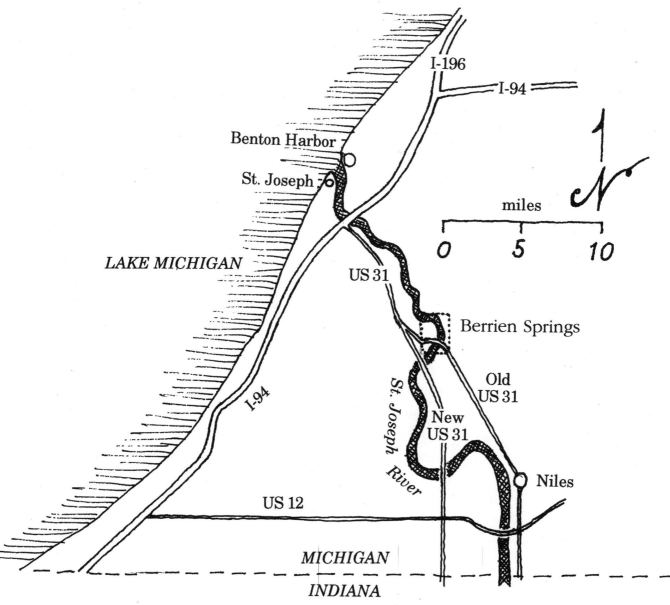

The barn with its area for hiding slaves and the
elaborate seed storage facility are gone.

For two years, Joseph Snyder served as the agent. Then from 1865 to 1868, Levi Shaw, a trustee of the North Family at Mount Lebanon, directed the operation. A newspaper account describes Shaw's frequent visits to Berrien Springs indicating that "he was well known in the village."[5]

Berrien Springs residents remembered the flourishing days from 1865 to 1873 when John P. Vedder was the farm's overseer. "He was a good spender, had a large family of children and relatives, and employed during the season perhaps 50 men and twenty or thirty horses in carrying on the farm and seed-growing operations."[6] In 1866 Vedder received one-third of the production of the farm. The Shakers paid for improvements and insurance on the buildings and their outlay was $2,000 more than their income that year.[7]

By 1870, it was noted that 250 acres of the farm were improved. The livestock included six horses, nine milch cows, 22 other cattle, 46 sheep, and nine swine. Eleven hundred bushels of winter wheat, 50 bushels of Indian corn, 50 bushels of oats, 25 bushels of buckwheat, 11 bushels of peas and beans, and 150 bushels of Irish potatoes were harvested that year. They produced 1,600 pounds of butter and sold 30 gallons of milk.[8]

Farm management at a distance produced some problems. In November 1861, 1,100 bushels of wheat and 2,000 bushels of corn came from Michigan, but the cost of the freight was $1,000. Elder Frederick Evans, intensely interested in agriculture, noted that wheat from their Michigan farm had sold for just $2 a bushel; later they had to buy wheat for $3 a bushel. In exasiration he asserted, "We have always missed it in selling our wheat."[9]

In March 1873 the Shakers sold this farm to Shelton B. Shepard of Niles, Michigan, in exchange for two houses and lots in Niles, Michigan (at the corner of Second and Sycamore Streets) and four houses and lots in Chicago, owned by Shepard and Francis W. Gray.[10] The effort of maintaining a farm so far from home base by a diminishing number of Shakers was taking its toll. At the same time it was divesting this Michigan farm, the North Family at New Lebanon was adding a sawmill and three acres to its recent acquisition of hundred of acres around Windsor, New York, an investment closer to home.

In evaluating the ownership of the Shaker farm at Berrien Springs, Elder Evans noted that "it made us much trouble." He indicated that each person who was put in charge caused the community a loss. There was an effort to run the farm: "We built a barn, repaired and painted fences, built a windmill." But the farm was sold and the Shakers took buildings and lots in exchange which Evans suggested were "a Bill of cost in no income from first to last."[11]

The Shaker farm at Berrien Springs became a dairy farm after World War II; however the landscape has changed since then. The 250-acre flood plain, owned by Andrews University, still produces a good corn crop. The barn with its area for hiding slaves and the elaborate seed storage facility are gone. George Kimmel's home remains on four acres of the Shaker farm. Owners Scott and Mary Ellen Pluss, 8930 Shaker Farm Road, Berrien Springs, Michigan 49103, suggest contacting them if you would like to visit the farm. You will need specific directions to get there. A residential area has developed near the farmhouse on the bluffs above the river.

[1] *North Family Book of Records*, New York Public Library, Astor, Lenox and Tilden Foundations, Manuscripts and Archives Division, Shaker Manuscript No. 20, 65.

[2] Gordon Gray, *My Family and I.* (Chicago: R. R. Donnelley & Sons Co., 1964), 4.

[3] Rose R. Burket, "The Underground Railroad in Berrien County," from the files of the Maude Preston Palenske Library, St. Joseph, Michigan, 4.

[4] Schedule, Productions of Agriculture in Oronoko Township, County of Berrien, Michigan, 1860.

[5] "Shaker Farm, Berrien Springs, has History," *News Palladium*, St. Joseph, Michigan, January 5, 1920.

[6] Ibid.

[7] *North Family Book of Records*, 75.

[8] Schedule, Productions of Agriculture in Oronoko Township, County of Berrien, Michigan, 1870.

[9] Frederick Evans, ["*Cares & Burthens. . .*"], The Edward Deming Andrews Memorial Shaker Collection, The Winterthur Library, 1861-1892, n.p.

[10] *The North Family Book of Records* indicates that the Shakers sold the Berrien Springs farm to Francis M. Gray; the deeds, however, show that Shepard sold the farm to Gray in 1875 for one dollar. Perhaps they were rearranging their financial relationships. County tax records list "Shepard & Gray" for 1874; F.M. Gray, for 1875.

[11] Evans, *Mount Lebanon Journal*, 1861-1892, part of a section called "Blunders and Failures," n.d.

Unfinished Business

The farm at Berrien Springs was not the only investment the New Lebanon, New York, Shaker community made in Michigan. Their journals recount the acquisition of 320 acres of pine timber land in Saint Joseph, Berrien County, in 1853. The Center and North Families shared the cost of $1,900. In November 1858 the North Family purchased an additional 80 acres containing "black walnut and white wood, etc." adjacent to the first parcel. They paid $1,000 for it.[1] Acquisitions by the New Lebanon Shakers expressed the group's hopes for additional land investments to provide for their future prosperity.

It was not long, however, before the scarcity of Shakers who could hold positions of trust and care made them absentee landlords. This caused a loss of control and profits. In 1866 Benjamin Gates and Robert Valentine, trustees for the Church Family at Mount Lebanon, sold a half section (360 acres) of land in Gratiot County to Evan M. Potter.[2] This land is north of Lansing, Michigan. The sales of land continued into the 1870s. In 1871, a small parcel of Michigan land sold for $150. In May 1872 the 80-acre farm near Saint Joseph was sold.

In July 1877 the North Family traded again with Francis Gray. This time they exchanged the houses and lots in Niles and their half of the pine farm near Saint Joseph for additional lots in Chicago. Later Gray served as an agent for the Shakers, agreeing to sell all their Illinois and Michigan land still owned by the North Family. By 1881 Grant, Swift and Company was employed to supervise the Chicago lots. Less than a month later, a claim was leveled against the Chicago land, which caused the North Family much trouble. Elder Frederick Evans noted, "We took [the] Chicago lots twice each time a blunder nothing but loss as yet."[3]

Then in July 1885 the North Family at Mount Lebanon lost the note due on the Michigan pine lot near Saint Joseph. The journal writer lamented the fact that the note was taken without security.[4] Clearly it was a burden to manage these far-flung properties.

The documentation for most of these Michigan and Illinois purchases is primarily in Mt. Lebanon journal entries. It is a challenge to verify these transactions in county deeds. Land transactions in Michigan are listed by the names of the trustees representing the Shaker community. Niles, Saint Joseph, and Berrien Springs are all in Berrien County; but not all the deeds for the land transactions chronicled in the *Mount Lebanon Journal* were located in the Berrien County Record of Deeds office.

Other Shaker communities were also involved in land acquisitions in the nineteenth century. During the 1820s the Watervliet, New York, community acquired a farm of 167 acres in Hudson, Illinois, from Reuben Treadway, a member from 1822 to 1829. The Shakers inspected the property in 1855 and had a house and barn built there; they also hired a manager for the farm. By 1857 Watervliet was getting wheat from Illinois. Generally one of their trustees went out each year to check the operation.[5]

We learned that Hudson is in McLean County near Bloomington, but the county recorder was unable to locate any land owned by Reuben Treadway or the Shakers. Another researcher said that McLean County was organized in 1830 from Tazewell County, which was organized in 1827 from Sangamon County, which was organized in 1821 from the Northwest Territory. Sangamon County records are located in Springfield, Illinois.

Other farms in Illinois proved equally elusive. The Shaker Museum at Old Chatham, New York, has a Church Family record from Watervliet, New York, in which a Declaration of Chancery lists two farms in Cook County, Illinois.[6] One farm of 240 acres was sold by Allen Denny and Polly, his wife, to Chauncey Miller and Chauncey Copley, Watervliet trustees, on May 15, 1860. An additional 160 acres in Cook County were sold to Chauncey Miller and Jesse Harwood, trustees, on June 3, 1864, by Isaac and Mary Holloway. County records of these acquisitions were destroyed in the Great Chicago Fire of 1873.

The same Declaration of Chancery lists other tracts acquired by Watervliet in Kentucky. In January 1865 the Church Family acquired 2,955 acres in Morgan County, as well as 365 acres in Magoffin County. In August 1866 they purchased a whopping 25,117 acres in Rowan County. These tracts were described as "wilderness land" in Kentucky. The counties are located in the northeastern part of the state. The area supports small family farms; tobacco crops are important to the economy. The land acquisitions seem highly speculative.

Land along the Kankakee River in LaPorte County, Indiana, chronicled in Union Village journals, does not appear in the deeds at the LaPorte County Recorder's Office.

So the loose ends continue to tantalize and the adventure continues...

1 *North Family Book of Records*, New York Public Library, Astor, Lenox and Tilden Foundations, Manuscripts and Archives Division, Shaker Manuscript No. 20, 58 and 64.

2 Description in the deed: East half of Section 26, Township 10 North Range One West.

3 Frederick Evans, ["*Cares & Burthens*. . ."], The Edward Deming Andrews Memorial Shaker Collection, The Winterthur Library, 1861-1892, n.p.

4 Ibid.

5 Letter to the author from Elizabeth Shaver, March 16, 1996.

6 Church Family vol. 232, *Book of Records* [Watervliet, NY] No. 2, 1814-1915, The Shaker Museum and Library, Old Chatham, New York, 249-50.

Appendix I

Last Will and Testament of Springfield Presbytery

The Presbytery of Springfield, sitting at Cane-ridge, in the county of Bourbon, being through a gracious Providence, in more than ordinary bodily health, growing in strength and size daily; and in perfect soundness and composure of mind, but knowing that it is appointed for all delegated bodies once to die; and considering that the life of every such body is very uncertain, do make, and ordain this our last Will and Testament, in a manner and form following, viz:

Imprimis. We *will*, that this body die, be dissolved, and sink into union with the Body of Christ at large; for there is but one body, and one Spirit, even as we are called in one hope of our calling.

Item. We *will*, that our name of distinction with its Reverend title be forgotten, that there be but one Lord over God's heritage, and his name one.

Item. We *will* that our power of making laws for the government of the church, and executing them by delegated authority, forever cease; that the people may have free course to the Bible, and adopt the law of the Spirit of life in Christ Jesus.

Item. We *will*, that candidates for the Gospel ministry henceforth study the Holy scripture with fervent prayer, and obtain license from God to preach the simple Gospel, with the Holy Ghost sent down from heaven, without any mixture of philosophy, vain deceit, traditions of men, or the rudiments of the world. And let none henceforth take this honor to himself, but he that is called of God, as was Aaron.

Item. We *will*, that the church of Christ resume her native right of internal government—try her candidates for the ministry, as to their soundness in the faith, acquaintance with experimental religion, gravity and aptness to teach; and admit no proof of their authority but Christ speaking in them. We will, that the church of Christ look up to the Lord of the harvest to send forth laborers into his harvest; and that she resume her primitive right trying those who say they are apostles, and are not.

Item. We *will*, that each particular church, as a body, actuated by the same spirit choose her own preacher, and support him by a free will offering, without a written call or subscription—admit members—remove offences; and never henceforth delegate her right of government to any man or set of men whatever.

Item. We *will*, that the people henceforth take the Bible as the only sure guide to heaven; and as many as are offended with other books, which stand in competition with it, may cast them into the fire if they choose; for it is better to enter into life having one book, than having many to be cast into hell.

Item. We *will*, that preachers and people, cultivate a spirit of mutual forbearance, pray more and dispute less; and while they behold the signs of the times, look up, and confidently expect, that redemption draweth nigh.

Item. We *will*, that our weak brethren, who may have been wishing to make the Presbytery of Springfield their king, and wot not what is now become of it, betake themselves to the Rock of Ages, and follow Jesus for the future.

Item. We *will* that the Synod of Kentucky examine every member who may be suspected of having departed from the Confession of Faith, and suspend every such suspected heretic immediately; in order that the oppressed may go free, and taste the sweets of gospel liberty.

Item. We *will*, that Ja____ _____, the author of two letters lately published in Lexington, be encouraged in his zeal to destroy partyism. We will, moreover, that our past conduct be examined into by all who may have correct information; but let foreigners beware of speaking evil of things which they know not.

Item. Finally we *will*, that our all our sister bodies read their Bibles carefully, that they may see their fate there determined, and prepare for death before it is too late.

Springfield Presbytery
June 28, 1804   L. S.
Robert Marshall, B.W. Stone, John Dunlavy, John Thompson,
Richard M'Namar, David Purviance
Witnesses.

From Elder John Rogers' *The Biography of Eld. Barton Warren Stone* (Cincinnati: Published for the author by J.A. & U.P. James), 1847, 51-55.

Appendix II

Names from Cabin Creek, Kentucky
From South Union **Record A.**

Dickson, James
Dickson, S.
McGehan, Alexander
McGehan, Sally

McGigham, A.
Waite, Richard
Waite, Reuben

Names from Paint Lick, Kentucky
From South Union **Record A.**

Adams, Elijah
Bishop, Sally
Bruner, Anne
Carns, William
Coons, Rachel
Harris, Benjamin
Harris, Samuel
Harris, Betsy
Houston, Fanny
Houston, Matthew
Houston, Peggy
Hutton, Betsy
Hutton, Hannah
Hutton, Henry

Hutton, Rachel
Maxwell, John
Maxwell, Sally
McCarver, Joseph
McCarver, Betsy
McNelly, Rebecca
Shields, Joel
Shields, Polly
Shields, Sally
Thomas, Polly
Thomas, Sally
Woodrum, Drura
Woods, John

Names from Eagle Creek and Straight Creek, Ohio
from J.P. MacLean's **Shakers of Ohio,** *South Union*
Record A, *Deeds and Local Histories.*

Boyles, Jenny
Brownfield, James
Brown, Andrew (moved to UV)
Burns, Alexander
Burns, David
Burns, Jenny- (moved to UV)
Carr, Anna (young sister)
Caspy (Cospey), Joseph
Clark, Nancy
Clark, William
Conft, Ebin

Daves, Nicholas
Devoe, Nicholas
Dragoo, Andrew
Dragoo, Belteshazzer (wife Hannah)
Dragoo, Belteshazzer (wife Martha)
Dragoo, Betty- moved to UV
Duncan, Nancy (wife of James)
Dunlavy, Anthony
Dunlavy, Betsy (daughter of John)
Dunlavy, Cassia (wife of John)
Dunlavy, John

Dunlavy, Nancy
Eddie (Edie), Peggy
Eddie, David
Edgington, John (wife Polly)
Gallaghar, Adam (son of William)
Gallagher, Betsy
Gallagher, Jane (dau. of William)
Gallagher, Nancy (dau. of William)
Gallaghar, Rebecca
Gallaghar (Gollaher), William
Gates, Reuben- family moved to UV
Hall, Edward (wife believes, but he
    is outraged)
Hall, Elijah
Hall, Mary
Hodkins, Betsy
Hodkins, James
Hubert, Catherine
Hughey (Hughye, Hughy), Alexander
Johnson, John (wife Martha)
Johnson, Joseph
Kallaghan, Thomas
Kitchell, Ashbell
Knox, Brown F.E.
Knox, Easter (or Easther)
Knox, John
Knox, Peggy (young sister)
Knox, William (wife Agnes)
Knox, William (wife Nancy)
Legier, George (wife Elizabeth)
Martin, Fielding
McCowley (McCauley), Henry
McGehan (McKehan), Alexander
McGehan, Sally
McNemar, Garner (Richard's brother)

McNemar, Betsy (Garner's wife)
McNemar, John (Garner's son)
Miller, Daniel
Miller, John
Moore, Sally
Moore, Amos
Moore, William (a young man)
Morris, Reuben (family moved to UV)
Mosely, Daniel
Nailor, John-(Naylor) SC to UV
Naylor, Richard
Painter, Jonas
Painter, Joseph
Pangburn, H.
Pangburn, Peggy
Pointer, Jo
Rankin, Daniel
Redman, Dave
Redmond, S.
Scott, Nancy (19 yrs old in 1810)
Sharp, Eliza
Sharp, Elizabeth
Sharp, John- Straight Creek, went to
UV
Sharp, Molly (sister of William)-SC
Sharp, Nathan (son of John)
Sharp, Polly
Sharp, William (Straight Creek)
Shaw
Shriezes (Shrizes, Shreeves), Jonas
Vance, Thomas
Wate, Reuben
White, Jenny (w. of William)
White, William, (h. of Jenny)

Names from Busro or West Union
From J.P. MacLean's Shakers of Ohio

Anderson, Thomas
Bates, Elder Issachar
Beard, Thos.
Bedell, Hortency
Bennet, Joseph
Bennet, Pelly

Bennet, Polly
Bowles, Zecharia
Boyls (Boyles), Charles
Boyls (Boyles), Nancy
Boyls (Boyles), Rebecca
Brazzleton, William

Brazzleton, Rebecca
Brownfield. James
Daily, John
Darrow, Eldress Ruth
Davis, Enoch
Davis, James
Davis, Lovina
Davis, Rachel
Dennis, Eldress Saloma
Dennis, William
Douglass, Jonathan
Douglas, William- trustee
Duncan, James
Duncan, Rachel
Edgington, Israel
Edgington, John
Edgington, John Jr.
Edgington, Joseph
Edgington, Magia (daughter of John Polly
Edgington, Polly
Edie, Ascenath
Edie, David
Edie, Polly
Edie, Ruth
Evans, James
Farrington, Mother Ruth
Ford, Charles
Ford, Henry M.
Ford, John II
Ford, Mary Ann
Ford, Peggy
Ford, Dr. Robert
Ford, Robert
Fowler, Chester
Fowler, John
Fowler, Nancy
France, Brittanna
France, Claricy
Gallagher, Adam- trustee
Gallagher, Rebecca
Gallagher, William
Gill, Benjamin
Gill, Isabella
Gill, Nancy
Gill, Robert
Hadden, Davis- a black man
Hadden, John
Hall, Ann
Hall, Nancy

Hall, Rachel
Handcock, Anny
Hancock, John
Hansborough (Hansbury), Smith
Harris, William
Hill, Anne
Hill, William and Betsy
Hopkins, James- trustee
Hopkins, Mary- North Family eldress
Houston, Betsy
Houston, Jenny
Houston, Robert
Houston, William
Hutcheson, John
James, Betsy
James, William
Jenkins, Betsy
Jenkins, Nancy
Jenkins, Olive
Jenkins, Sally
Jenkins, Sarah,
Jinkins, James
Johnson, John
Johnston, John
Johnston, Joseph
Johnston, Martha
Johnston, Samuel- trustee
Jones, Abraham- a colored man
Kinkly, Mark
Kirkindall, Adam
Knox, Benjamin
Knox, Esther
Knox, John
Knox, Nancy
Knox, Peggy
Knox, William
Knox, William Jr.
Latham, Catharine
Latham, Julia
Lathom, David
Laycock, Sally
Legier, Amy
Legier, George- land deacon
Legier, Jesse
Legier, Noah
Lockwood, Joseph
Martin, Jane
Martin, John
McClelland, Samuel

McComb, Betsy
McComb, Elizabeth
McComb, John
McComb, Lucy
McComb, Nancy
McComb, Ruth
McComb, Sally
McKeen, Betsy
McKeen, Jesse
McKeen, Margary
McKeen, Samuel
McReynold, Leonard- from Red Banks, Ky.
Meacham, Elder Archibald
Mead, James
Miller, Henry- North Family elder
Miller, John
Miller, Lucinda
Miller, Naomi (sister of John Dunlavy)
Moore, William
Murphy, Betsy
Murphy, Phebe
Naulin Leoden
Naylor, Eldress Patience
Neeley, James
Newlin, James
Newlin, Polly
Page, Oremsted- a colored man
Pegg, Nathan
Pegg, Ruth
Price, Benjamin
Price, David
Price, Fanny
Price, James
Price, Rebecca
Price, William
Rankin, Daniel
Redmon, Daniel
Redmond, William

Roberts, Elijah
Roberts, Joseph
Roberts, Martha
Roberts, Peggy
Roberts, Salome
Roberts, William
Roberts, William Jr.
Royce, Frederic W.
Rubart, Elizabeth
Sanford, Eldress Martha
Shaw, James
Shaw, Joseph
Shaw, Mary
Shermon, Amelia
Sherman, Anna
Sherman, Manly
Sherman, Ezra Jr.
Sherman, Ezra Sr.
Shreeves, Martha
Shreeves, Jonah
Slover, Eunice
Slover, John
Slover, John Jr.
Slover, Luanna
Sparks, Pheby
Stewart, Peggy
Stroud, Betsy
Stroud, Indiana
Stroud, Louisiana
Stroud, Reece
Tann, Anthony- a black man
Tann, Peggy (Anthony's wife, a white woman)
Worthington, Betsy
Worthington, Nancy
Worthington, Joseph
Worthington, Samuel
Youngman, John

Names from Darby Plains
From J.P. MacLean's *Shakers of Ohio*
and Agnes A. Arnold's "From Rice City, R.I. to Ohio"

Bacon, Elijah
Bates, Archibald L.-didn't become a Shaker
Brownell, Gideon
Burlingame, Emma
Burlingame, Nathan
Burnham, Almira
Burnham, Polly
Burnham, William
Burnham, Zilpha
Champlain, Polly
Champlain, Susan
Clark, Polly
Easterbrooks, John
Easterbrooks, Lucy
Farnum, Douglas
Farnum, Louisa (Douglas' daughter)
Farnam, Susanna (Douglas' wife)
Hathaway, Dr. Nicholas- a Farnhamite

Henman, Sarepta
Rice, Caleb
Rice, Ebenezer (son of Samuel)
Rice, Harriet Patrick (Samuel Jr's wife)-
    didn't become a Shaker
Rice, Jefferson
Rice, Lucy (Samuel Sr's wife)
Rice, Mariah
Rice, Sally Bates (Ebenezer's wife)-
    didn't become a Shaker
Rice, Samuel Jr
Rice, Samuel Sr
Simmons, Martin
Simmons, Charlotte
Thompson, James
Wells, Dorcas
Wells, James

Appendix III

The Survey Plotter and Virginia Military Survey 5708
Union County, Ohio

For this publication deed research was undertaken to determine the precise location of Shaker lands at Eagle Creek, White Oak Creek, Straight Creek, Red Oak Creek, Clinton County, Darby Plains, South Union, and Berrien Springs. In order to expedite the analysis, a computer program was developed which converts the deed descriptions of directions and distances of property lines bounding any rectilinear tract into scale plots of the tract's shape.[1]

Input data for the program are bearings expressed in decimal degrees and distances expressed in paces, rods, poles, feet, meters, or chains. Once these data have been entered, the program proceeds to draw the tract and compute its area in square feet, square meters or acres. Not only is the drafting process efficient, our experience indicates that errors may occur in the process of recording deeds in the county clerk's offices. For example, a bearing might really be North 40 degrees West whereas a scribe might enter N 40 E. Such errors, difficult to recognize from written descriptions alone, become easier to spot when a tract drawing crosses back on itself or fails significantly to close at the beginning station.

Most of the early land surveys in the Virginia Military District were written as metes and bounds. Here is a description of Virginia Military Survey 5708 in Union Township, Union County, Ohio, dated February 27, 1808:

> *Beginning at four Elms, Northeast corner to an Entry made for said Galloway No. 5130, and most Northerly corner to Robert Means' Survey No. 5265, running N. 85 W. 150 poles to two Bur Oaks and a Hickory; Thence N. 50 W. 40 poles to two Hickories and a Bur Oak; Thence S. 40 W. 40 Poles to two Elms; Thence N. 82 W. 180 poles to three Bur Oaks in the edge of a prairie; Thence S. 8 W. 90 poles to a Stake in a prairie; Thence S. 50 E. 44 poles, crossing the Creek at 8 poles, to a Stake in a prairie; Thence N. 80 E. 240 poles to a stake in the prairie; Thence S. 5 E. 20 poles to two Black Oaks; Thence S. 85 E. 150 poles to a Stake in a prairie in the line of said Means' Survey; Thence with his line N. 5 W. 100 poles, crossing the Creek at 20 poles, to the beginning.*

Without drawing even a simple sketch, it's hard to visualize that the above tract has a shape rather like a spread eagle in flight, spans over 200 acres, and fails to close by roughly 477 feet. To help you with your own diagram, a pole is equal to a rod or 16.5 feet.

A tract's shape and corner descriptions help determine where the tract lies in relation to adjacent tracts and local terrain features. The process is much like fitting pieces into a jigsaw puzzle.

In Survey 5708 we found two tracts that Douglas Farnum owned, one of 25 acres, and the other of 100 acres, as well as a part of the survey belonging to Samuel Rice with an unspecified number of acres. The 100-acre tract which Farnum owned looked as if it would fill the eastern part of the survey and include an early schoolhouse site on Route 4 where the Farnhamites might have met for worship.

The survey plotter revealed that the 98.5-acre eastern portion of a more accurate deed description of Survey 5708 completed in 1811 came close to having the bearings of Farnum's 100-acre tract. There was a problem, however. Dale Covington patiently wrote, "Unfortunately the distances as written in the deed have the long sides of the parallelogram-shaped tract running generally N-S, not E-W. The tract as recorded in the deed can neither start in the SW corner of tract 2 [the 25-acre tract of Farnum's] nor fit in Section 5708."

The longer we worked, the more mystified we became. Douglas Farnum sold this 100 acres in May 1818 to Asa Bates of Coventry, Rhode Island, about nine months after purchasing it. The deed also listed Elder Farnum as residing in the town of Coventry. Perhaps

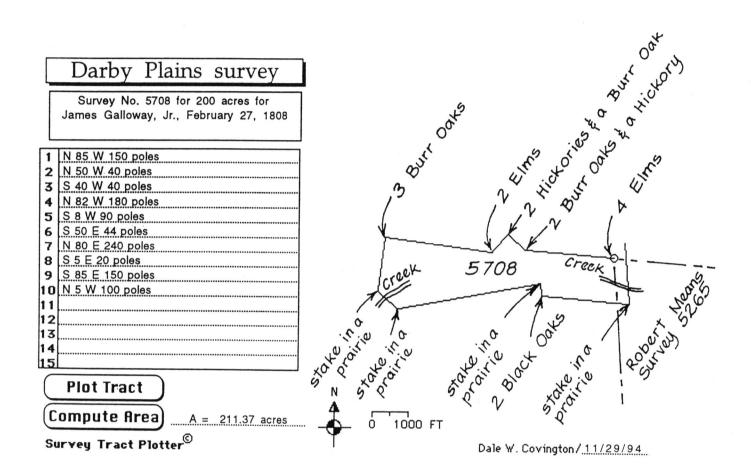

Darby Plains survey

Survey No. 5708 for 200 acres for James Galloway, Jr., February 27, 1808

1	N 85 W 150 poles
2	N 50 W 40 poles
3	S 40 W 40 poles
4	N 82 W 180 poles
5	S 8 W 90 poles
6	S 50 E 44 poles
7	N 80 E 240 poles
8	S 5 E 20 poles
9	S 85 E 150 poles
10	N 5 W 100 poles
11	
12	
13	
14	
15	

Plot Tract

Compute Area   A = 211.37 acres

Survey Tract Plotter©

Dale W. Covington / 11/29/94

he was trying to raise money to keep the group in Ohio solvent, promising his land if all else failed.

On April 29, 1819, the land in which the 100-acre tract was located was surveyed for Joshua Poythress. It became part of a 1,024-acre tract patented to him by President James Monroe on November 15, 1820. That swept away Bates' claim to the land.

After Farnum's death in 1822, Asa Bates, by then living in Windham, Connecticut, appointed his son, Cranston, as his attorney "to recover. . .debts due to me and all Claims and Demands. . . against Douglas Fornum Late of the State of Ohio. . ." A search of Madison and Union County deeds failed to turn up a sale of this land. Asa Bates was left holding an empty bag.

A breakthrough in understanding the correct relationship between the 100-acre

Darby Plains survey

Composite plot based in some instances on <u>interpretations</u> of deed descriptions for lands in Section 5708, Madison County, OH.

1. Land deeded to Samuel Rice by David Clover, deed Book 4, p. 25, April 6, 1818.

2-3. Quit claim deeded to Samuel Rice by Douglas Farnum, Vol. 1, p. 180, Nov. 28, 1821. location of tract 3 with respect to tract 2 approximately as shown, however location of combined tracts unclear. Originally tract 3, many of its dimensions unspecified, was deeded to Farnum by Rice in deed Book 3, p. 178, 27 [sic?] Aug 1817.

4. This tract contains about 98.5 a. and comes closest to having the <u>bearings</u> of the 100 a. tract described in land deeded to Farnum by Clover in deed Book 3, p. 179, Aug. 7 [sic?], 1817. Unfortunately the distances as written in the deed have the long side of the parallelogram-shaped tract running generally N-S, not E-W. The tract as recorded in the deed can neither start in the SW corner of tract 2 nor fit in Section 5708.

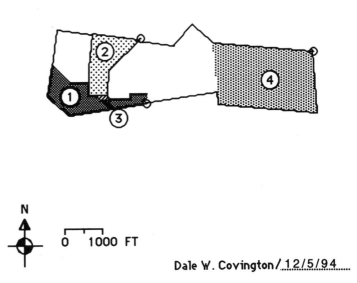

N

0   1000 FT

Dale W. Covington / 12/5/94

tract and the 25-acre tract occurred as more deeds were analyzed which abutted these tracts. Often these deeds had their own imperfections. For example, one key deed includes the vague phrase, "Thence Westwardly and Northwardly with the Meanders of Nicholas Hathaways land to the beginning." Gradually information on grantors, grantees, dates, corners, tract shapes and acreages all merged into a clearer, self-consistent picture of land transactions in this section of Union County.

No wonder the group from Union County and Champaign County who became Shakers were concerned about the titles to land in a military district.

Darby Plains survey

Composite plot based on deed descriptions for lands in or adjacent to Survey 5708, Madison County, OH, owned by those associated with the Darby Plains Shakers.

1. Land deeded to Samuel Rice by David Clover, Madison Co. deed Book 4, p. 25, 6 Apr 1818.

2-3. Quit claim deeded to Samuel Rice by Douglas Farnum, Vol. 1, p. 180, Nov. 28, 1821. Tract 3, many of its dimensions unspecified, was deeded to Farnum by Rice in deed Book 3, p. 178, 27 [sic?] Aug 1817. Tracts 1, 2 and 3 sold by Rice to Harriet Rice on 4 Dec 1824 who in turn sold this land to Nicholas Hathaway on 21 Dec 1824. See Union Co. deed Book 2, p. 98.

4. Land owned by Douglass Farnum from 1817 until he sold it to Asa Bates on 13 May, 1818, Madison Co. OH, deed Book 4, p. 35.

5. Inferred location of land that Samuel Rice purchased from Generals Taylor and Little. These deed records appear to be lost.

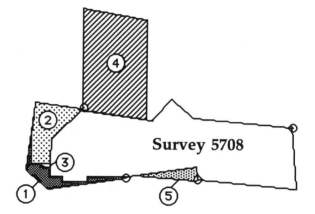

Survey 5708

John Easterbrooks' house was either at tract 3 or approximately 470 ft SE of tract 3.

N

0   1000 FT

Dale W. Covington / 2/23/95

[1] Dale W. Covington, Survey Tract Plotter, 1994, (unpublished). The software program, "Deed Mapper," has similar capabilities.

Further Reading

Burress, Marjorie Byrnside. *Whitewater, Ohio, Village of Shakers, 1824-1916: Its History and Its People.* Cincinnati: published by the author, 1979.

Clark, Thomas D., and Gerald F. Ham. *Pleasant Hill and Its Shakers.* Pleasant Hill, Kentucky: Shakertown Press, 1968, 2d ed., 1983.

Conlin, Mary Lou. *The North Union Story.* 1961. Reprint, Shaker Heights, Ohio: Shaker Historical Society, 1974.

Edwards, Sharon. "Population Characteristics and Trends of the Shaker Community of Union Village, Ohio, 1805-1870." *The Old Northwest* 14, no. 1 (1988):67-90.

Emlen, Robert P. *Shaker Village Views.* Hanover, New Hampshire: University Press of New England, 1987.

Hunt, Melba L. *"Summers at Watervliet"* Kettering, Ohio: Kettering-Moraine Museum and Historical Society, 1985.

Kilty, Klare Kay. "A Survey of the Origin of the Shaker Movement." Heritage Room, James White Library, Andrews University, Berrien Springs, Michigan, 1960.

Klyver, Richard D. *Brother James: The Life and Times of Shaker Elder James Prescott.* Shaker Heights, Ohio: The Shaker Historical Society, 1992.

MacLean, J. P. *Shakers of Ohio: Fugitive Papers Concerning the Shakers of Ohio, With Unpublished Manuscripts.* 1907. Reprint, Philadelphia: Porcupine Press, 1975.

McNemar, Richard. *The Kentucky Revival.* 1807. Reprint, New York: AMS Press, 1974.

Murray, Stuart. *Shaker Heritage Guidebook.* Spencertown, New York: Golden Hill Press, Inc., 1994.

Neal, Julia. *By Their Fruits: The Story of Shakerism in South Union, Kentucky.* 1947. Reprint, Philadelphia: Porcupine Press, 1975.

_____ *The Kentucky Shakers.* Lexington: The University Press of Kentucky, 1982.

Piercy, Caroline, and Arthur Tolve. *The Shaker Cookbook: Recipes & Lore from the Valley of God's Pleasure.* Bowling Green, Ohio: Gabriel's Horn Publishing Co., 1984.

Phillips, Hazel Spencer. *Richard the Shaker.* Lebanon: published by the author, 1972.

_____ *Shakers in the West.* Reprint of *Philadelphia Museum Bulletin*, Spring 1962.

Stein, Stephen J. *The Shaker Experience in America.* New Haven: Yale University Press, 1992.

The Contributors

Martha H. Boice provided the research for the lesser known Shaker sites and kept the project focused on the finish line. She lives with her husband Bill in Dayton, Ohio, where she became fascinated by the number of Daytonians who were unaware of the Shaker community in their midst called Watervliet. A Phi Beta Kappa graduate of Ohio Wesleyan University and the University of Michigan School of Social Work, Martha's particular pleasure is getting all the puzzle pieces to fit into place. Her family includes three grown children and two grandsons who encourage her with her projects. Historic preservation and herb gardening are her two areas of expertise.

Dale W. Covington's "gift" is his ability to use his computer in creative ways, putting facts and figures together in unique combinations. Educated in the disciplines of electrical engineering and nuclear engineering, Dale earned a B.S.E.E. from Vanderbilt University, a D.A.S.S. from Manchester University [Fulbright Scholar], an S.M. from M.I.T. and a Ph.D. from Georgia Tech. As a senior research engineer at Georgia Tech, Dale conducted contract sponsored research. He has written over 40 publications in the fields of electromagnetics, solid state physics, and Shakers in the west. Dale resides in Marietta, Georgia, and has a consummate interest in the Shaker outreach at White Oak, Georgia.

Richard B. Spence has been creating maps and drawings of Shaker buildings for many years. He has B.S. and M.B.A. degrees from Indiana University and augments his artistic and historic pursuits with his job as Human Resources Manager for United Air Specialists, Inc. in Cincinnati. Richard spent two years performing basic historical research for the Hamilton County Park District on the White Water Shakers. For the Warren County Historical Society, he created a panoramic sketch of Union Village which is displayed in the Robert and Virginia Jones Shaker Gallery at the museum. Richard, who lives with his wife Suzy in Cincinnati, indicates his ongoing interests are White Water and Shaker agricultural architecture.

Index

A transcript of the handwritten text found on
the inside front and back covers

A short account of the Situation of our Bethren at Ohio or that part
that is called Miami—It is said to be about 19 and 18 Milles broad
on an average—and about 50 or 54 in Length From N to S The NE
and SW Corners are about in that course—It is Surrounded by four
Butiful rivers Leaving it a Square island. Except a Narrow istmas of
about 6 Mills accross—which devides the Corses of the two rivers Little
Miami and Mad river, Little miami runs on the East side and
Emties into the ohio at the SE Corner—Mad river runs on the N side
and emties into the Big miami river at NW corner—and Big miami
runs along the west side and emties into the ohio at the SW corner
and the ohio Betwen the two Miamies runs from East to west—
all this water Leaves a Butiful Levil country not Perfectly But
Sufficiently so—Nearly in the Center of which our Lot is fallen as
the first seat of the Gospel in this Land—
65 miles East from this is Eagle creek 12 miles from the river Ohio
To a Society of Believers about 65 in number—here John Muldavy [Dunlavy]
Lives—
About 20 miles North from this our firt seat is Bulah [Beulah] where
there is another Society of Believers, here John Steward Lives
          There is Said to be about 100 Believers, *1806
About 200 Miles South from the miami is Paintlick in Kentucky
wher there is a nother Society of Believer here Mathew Houston* Lives

About 18 or 20 miles Distant from this is another Society of Believers
(The Point fo [of] Compas unknown to me)
There is anothere Society about 50 miles west from Paintlick
I find by further enquiry that these 2 latter Societies lies
first which is in Danville, County of Mercer 20 miles
west northwest from Paintlick, here lives Samuel Bondas [Bonta]
and Elisha Thomas, Chief men,—
Still on about 50 miles from this lies the other in
the town of Shelba [Shelby]; about west by north from
Danville, here lives John Bondas; principal man
Brother to the afore said Samuel; Dutch men
The principal part of the Believers in kentucky live nearly
In the Center of the State—Some of them at Shaunyrun in
In Mercer county 23 miles SW & at Paintlick (or ruralmount
In Garrad county) 40 miles S of Lexington Danvill is betw
=een the two places—12 miles from the former and 20 miles
from the Latter   Lexington is said to be 38 Deg & 6 miN[utes]

N lat. & 85. & 8 [minutes] west [longitude]— It is 90 miles South of the Ohio R
At ____ Cincinatia—& Cincinati is 30 m. SW of this—
Kentucky River runs from SE to NW & Lies between
the Believers & Lexington—Some of the Believers in Kentucky
In an E & W direction South of the River are scattered from
10 to 40 60 80 & some an hundred miles from each other.